FUNCTIONAL ASCETICISM

FUNCTIONAL ASCETICISM

A Guideline for American Religious

DONALD L. GELPI, S.J.

SHEED AND WARD : NEW YORK

✝

© Sheed and Ward, Inc., 1966

Imprimi Potest
John Edwards, S.J.
Provincial
New Orleans Province
Society of Jesus

Nihil Obstat
Thomas J. Beary
Censor Librorum

Imprimatur
† Robert F. Joyce
Bishop of Burlington
May 10, 1966

Library of Congress Catalog Card Number 66–22012

Manufactured in the United States of America

to the new and the old
breed alike:
together
they are the Church

PREFACE

THIS BOOK is in large measure the product of innumerable conversations with my fellow Jesuits and with religious of other orders and congregations. If, then, they find their own image reflected in these pages, it will not be by accident.

I wish to thank particularly C. J. McNaspy, S.J., for helping me in the writing of this book and for undertaking a critical introduction to it. His kindness in doing so only increases a debt of friendship already too large for me ever to repay.

I also wish to thank in a special way Gordon Saussy, S.J., Whitney Engeran, S.J., Lawrence Conlon, S.J., and Bruce Biever, S.J., for a series of discussions we shared concerning seminary training which provided the initial stimulus for the early chapters of this book. In addition I owe a debt of gratitude to John McMahon, S.J., Gordon George, S.J., Augustin Ellard, S.J., Joseph Fisher, S.J., Edwin Falteisek, S.J., James McNamara, S.J., and Eugene Cavanaugh, S.J., for reading either all or a portion of the manuscript and for generously taking from their time to provide many sound criticisms which have helped to make this a much better book than it would otherwise have been.

I would like also to caution the reader concerning the use of the word "nominalism" in the pages which follow. Every author has, I believe, the liberty to redefine terms, even traditional ones, to suit his purposes. The meaning of the term "nominalism" as I use it repeatedly in the pages which follow has nothing to do with classical nominalism of late medieval thought. It refers rather to a specific way of thinking about reality. "Nominalism" as I use the term here means nothing else than *the rigid substitution of one possible conceptualization of reality for the reality itself*. There is some danger of confusion on this point since I also suggest that in contemporary theologizing this way of thinking has its historical roots in the methods of positive theology, which was indeed the product of late scholasticism. My concern, however, is primarily with the existing reality of clerical and religious formation rather than with any academic evaluation of the late medieval nominalist-realist controversies. It is to be hoped that this is already clear from what follows; but explicit insistence on it here may possibly help to obviate some unnecessary misunderstandings.

Furthermore, any religious who would interpret functional asceticism as some sort of mandate for a religious subject to sit in solitary judgment upon every decision of his superiors and then to go his solitary way should those decisions fail to come up to his personal norms of excellence would have badly missed the point which I am trying, however inadequately, to make in the pages which

8

follow. To insist, as I do, upon the functional purpose of religious authority is in no way to deny that superiors do in fact have the "last say" when the moment comes for a final decision one way or another in the face of some concrete need or problem. But a functional approach to authority will, I believe, help to remind both subjects and superiors alike that in practical matters no "say" can truly claim to be the absolutely "last" one which does not solve the problem in hand or meet the existing need. Far from encouraging superiors and subjects to sit in judgment on one another, however, a functional approach to the exercise of authority in religion will, I hope, help to bind superiors and subjects more closely together *in proper subordination to one another precisely because of* their mutual devotion to a common apostolic purpose.

There is nothing "naturalistic" about such a conception of authority. The goals in question are always supernatural. The enterprise is a work of grace, and hence ultimately a work of God, not of man. But as long as God desires us to co-operate in the work of salvation, it is for us to see to it that we do so efficiently and expertly. Surely a work of grace demands no less, even though it does in fact demand much more.

Moreover, functional asceticism will, I believe, help American religious to realize that their quest for "personal perfection" is intimately bound up with their service of one another in faith and love and that the submission of my own will to another in obedience will aid me in my struggle against self-love to the extent that it effectively mediates my own love for others in the name of Christ.

I wish also to insist that the nominalistic mentality which I describe in the pages which follow is a mental construct and nothing else. It is *not* a description of any presently or previously existing persons or institutions. It is the effort to delineate *in the abstract* an attitude of mind which has, I believe, been operative *in varying degrees* in the training of seminarians and religious. As I describe it, it will no doubt be consciously rejected by any religious; but even so, it is an attitude which has, I fear, been *unconsciously and unthematically* operative in more of our thinking and activity than we may like at times to admit. My purpose in describing it is to help, if possible, to bring it to consciousness where it does exist in order that it may be dealt with appropriately. Nor is it my intention to suggest that this nominalistic mentality has been the only factor operative in the lives of religious in this country. Indeed, the whole point of the book is that a "functional" spirit is already operative in much of what we do as religious and that it is quite in conformity with the ideals of religious living.

Nevertheless, I have no intention of presenting a complete theology of the religious life in the pages which follow. Nor does functional asceticism pretend to be a complete program for religious renewal. What I am presenting to my fellow religious for their reflection is my own personal reflections on fifteen years in the religious life, nothing more, nothing less, in the hope that it may stimulate intelligent discussion of the problems of renewal which confront us all.

Finally, if I may do so without presumption, I would like to pay formal tribute to the dedicated efforts of all those in the American Church who are committed to the crucial work of effecting a responsible revitalization of religious life in this country. The pioneering efforts of movements like Sister Formation are a tribute to the conscientious zeal of men and women who had the vision to anticipate by several years the call to religious renewal only recently issued by Vatican II. The work of the Sister Formation Movement alone has already had considerable impact on the apostolic effectiveness of religious in this country. If this book can help in any way to further not only its efforts but also any similar attempt to bring about a responsible restructuring of American religious orders and congregations, it will have more than fulfilled the hopes and expectations of its author.

As the title of this book suggests, it is my hope that the personal reflections contained in it may through intelligent discussion help to serve as some sort of guideline for renewal among American religious. Hence, as a further practical aid to intelligent discussion, I have also included the chief guidelines for religious renewal officially set down in the documents of Vatican II. They appear in the form of an appendix to this book, even though the

11

book itself in no way pretends to be a formal commentary on the conciliar documents. Let me, however, hasten to add that I feel personally convinced that the functional asceticism which I here propose is in fact in radical continuity with the guidelines for renewal laid down by the bishops. I am particularly grateful to Walter Abbott, S.J., for his gracious permission to reprint the pertinent selections from the improved translation of the conciliar documents which appears in his excellent edition *The Documents of Vatican II* (America Press, 1966).

Our Lady of Martyrs Tertianship
Auriesville, New York
October, 1965

CONTENTS

CONTENTS

INTRODUCTION

IN THE JARGON of aggiornamento, asceticism can hardly class as an "in" word. Recent books on spirituality happily concentrate on grace, love, witness, commitment and liturgical attitudes. Indeed, a glance through the eighty-six columns that index *The Documents of Vatican II* discloses no mention of asceticism whatever. It would seem that the Fathers of the Council, in their concern to be positive and relevantly modern, declined to treat of anything so dour-sounding, so redolent of the ancient desert fathers or of those frightening Irish monks whose exploits used to edify and intimidate novices in the spiritual life.

This is not to say that asceticism itself is "out." In the Council's very first constitution, that *On the Sacred Liturgy,* we are austerely reminded that "before men can come to the liturgy they must be called to faith and to conversion," that "the Church must ever preach faith and repentance," that men must "repent and mend their ways." To have done otherwise would have been to be less than faithful to Christ, Who never minced words regarding the cross and the hard work required of His followers.

15

Functional Asceticism

Further, as we examine the Council documents, we discover that the entire Church renewal program outlined therein presupposes an expenditure of effort such as no previous council ever ventured to call for. Renewal, in fact, imposes discomfort, the abandonment of accustomed ways and styles, the stern quest of God's purpose at a time when mediocrity is seen as crass betrayal. This, of course, means asceticism of the most rigorous sort, even if the term is not used.

As the *Constitution on the Church* makes clear in Chapter 5, such asceticism is thus normal to the Christian life. "All of Christ's followers are invited and bound to pursue holiness and the perfect fulfillment of their proper state," we are reminded. And even those who live "in the world" and who "make use of this world" must heed the Apostle's warning not to "get bogged down in it." Again asceticism.

But within the Church there are those called to play a special role. Chapter 6 of this Constitution, as well as the entire *Decree on the Appropriate Renewal of the Religious Life,* deals at some length with those who are "called by God to practice the evangelical counsels" and to "devote themselves in a special way to the Lord." And for all its wondrous diversity throughout church history, religious life has always involved varying forms of asceticism adjusted to its varying function.

To a degree, this function has been undeviating in the course of salvation history: oneness with God, and after

16

the Incarnation, oneness with God in Christ. Not, to be sure, that the initiative comes from man, as Pelagians or Semi-Pelagians suppose. Christian asceticism, while by definition an "exercise," is never more than an exercise of response to God's summons—indeed, a graced response. And to that extent, the function of Christian asceticism (whether in religious life or not) has always been identical, whether the ascetic was Paul, Anthony, Augustine, Benedict, Bernard, Francis, Dominic, Ignatius or other. Yet the modality has always been diverse; the epoch that produced a Bonaventure produced an Aquinas; the century of Charles Borromeo is that of Philip Neri. As no two calls, so no two responses appear identical, save for what matters most. Part of the splendor of Christ's closest followers is their multiplicity, and we would be naive indeed to suppose that the possibilities have been exhausted.

Father Gelpi's book is in no sense designed as a full textbook of the spiritual life, as though to supplant the rich and growing literature on this subject. On the contrary, it presupposes that the reader, presumably someone with a good deal of experience with the religious state, knows what the spiritual life and asceticism mean. Instead, it grapples with a number of problems that trouble the sincere modern religious precisely because he is sincere, modern and religious. Anyone who is under middle age today has grown up in a world of exceptional complexity. To him, and to a degree to all of us, the ordinary tensions that are part of the human lot are now, if anything, more taut and wrenching than ever.

It has never been easy, even speculatively, to reconcile being in the world yet not of the world, or to reconcile authority with freedom, obedience with responsibility, detachment with authentic love, initiative with resignation, personal fulfillment with renunciation, the institutional with the charismatic. Nor has it ever been a simple task to discern means and ends, to separate essentials from frills, eternal principles from shifting, existential applications.

Every generation of religious has faced its vexing problems of adaptation—how to remain faithful to the seminal insight of the institute and its founder, while adjusting to ever divergent present needs. Every order or congregation that has survived (for not all have) has done so by keeping a fast grip on to its roots, while allowing for a dynamic expansion of concrete, immediate purposes. No one, however loyal to the holy rule, fancies that the Holy Spirit ceased to breathe once the initial impulse had been given.

Yet it would be disingenuous to pretend that today's problems in religious life are no more than copies of those of half a century ago or less. In an epoch of explosive communications, when ideas and ideals are instantly made available, no cloister is spiritually impenetrable. Still more, young people entering the novitiate or seminary today have been exposed to a far larger battery of influences than their elders; they have read more, traveled more, seen more, experienced more, shared more. More choices are open to them. They are, as Sargent Shriver described them, "reasonable, restless, questioning, challenging, taking nothing for granted." They expect more, and they do not change by simply donning a religious garb. Nor should we expect or wish them to. For this would be to attempt to shackle God's grace or coerce it into contrived channels. The venerable Thomistic adage about grace building on nature has not been found wanting.

Today's aspiring religious, even when he does not use the term, expects religious life to be functional; he is not easily reconciled to what appears dysfunctional. Not that he is less generous; my personal impression is that he is rather more so. But he knows of many ways of being generous. Witness the uncynical response to the Peace Corps, Vista and hundreds of volunteer service groups. Accordingly, he expects the form of religious life which he is to embrace or has already embraced to show its credentials, palpably and irrefutably. If, as the title of Chapter 1 implies, religious are at the crossroads, they want to know why.

In Chapter 2, "Nominalism and Asceticism," Father Gelpi offers us a most timely diagnosis. Formalism, juridicism, extrinsicism are among the pet bugaboos of today's finest youth, who see in them symptoms of what is popularly called phoneyness. Some of us older religious, eager to preserve fidelity to the Word and to the word of God as we have grasped it, have at times confused formulations with reality. We can do well to examine Father Gelpi's study of this danger, even if we find this chapter somewhat severely analytical. It will, I believe, repay the ascetical effort expended, and is, further, the key to later developments.

Whoever has read Father Gelpi's recent volume, *Life and Light: A Guide to the Theology of Karl Rahner,* especially pp. 197–207 on "The Religious Vocation," will need no further invitation to explore the present book. At the risk of being too obvious, I shall suggest that it seems geared principally to religious that are dedicated to the external apostolate—to "contemplatives in action," as the phrase goes. Yet it has much to say, too, both to enclosed contemplatives and to those directing future diocesan priests. In any case, the very concept *functional* indicates that adaptation must be made to each specific need, if the book is to be truly functional and not merely "nominalistic." One non-American friend who read the manuscript registered only a single complaint, which I quote here: "The peculiarly 'American' nature of the problem is questionable; it appears that the crisis of which Father Gelpi speaks transcends the American situation, and in fact that its American form is but a mild version of the way in which it is felt in other parts of the world." Whether or not this is so, possible translators will have to decide. But here in America I am confident that there are few religious, and probably no superiors, who will not find Father Gelpi's reflections probing, prodding and ultimately very helpful in this challenging post-conciliar age.

C. J. McNaspy, S.J.

I / RELIGIOUS AT THE CROSSROADS

1 / RELIGIOUS AT THE CROSSROADS

IF THE MEN AND WOMEN who came sailing over on the *Mayflower* had had any inkling of the full consequences of their voyage, it is a good guess that they would have turned back and gone home. Had you asked them at the time what they were about, they would have replied that they were the vanguard of the Protestant Reformation, summoned by God to realize the Protestant dream of a perfect society in a land where no papist kings could meddle in the business of God's saints. On the face of it they had every reason to believe that their dream could indeed be realized. But with human fallibility they had overlooked the joker hidden in the pack, the incalculable element which somehow their Ramist logic had failed to reckon with. That element was the land itself, the vast and challenging wilderness, which worked subtly upon their spirits to transform the Puritan religious idealist into the bustling Yankee pragmatist.

The Puritans were the first to undergo this unexpected metamorphosis, but they were far from being the last. There is a peculiar chemistry in the American soil which works upon transplanted European religious institutions to transform them in spite of themselves into something their continental ancestors never intended them to be. It is this same chemistry which has for centuries been at work in the American Catholic Church. The Catholicism which was in the Europe of our ancestors like a plant to be found in every garden became in America a hothouse bloom whose survival in an alien climate depended upon its gradual evolutionary transformation.

Like the Puritans themselves, Catholics were largely unconscious of the transformation going on within them. Isolated in a predominantly hostile religious environment, they clung to their old institutions as their only means of preserving any religious self-identity. Allegiance to Roman ways became the badge of an embattled Church; and so proudly was it worn that even as late as the opening of Vatican II many American Catholics were rudely shocked to discover that while the badge had remained the same over the centuries, they themselves had changed spiritually with the same subtle and inexorable chemistry that had transformed Puritan into Yankee. Not all of these changes have been necessarily for the better, and the problem of sorting them out and evaluating them is tremendously complex.

Moreover, what is true of American Catholicism in general has been equally true of American Catholic religious. Having attempted to lead the religious life both in this country and in Europe, I can testify personally to the fact of a genuine difference between the two. A

26

few examples may help illustrate what I mean. Shortly before embarking for Europe, I had occasion to see the movie *The Nun's Story*. Although I could not help admiring the film cinematically, I disturbed the people around me at several points with irrepressible fits of chuckling at what seemed to me a grotesque parody of the religious life I had lived and known. But I had not been in Belgium very long before I began to have second thoughts about the film. And by the end of a year I had come to the conclusion that it presented an almost documentary account of Belgian religious living. Another example: shortly before leaving Europe I happened to glance at a Catholic newspaper. There on the front page was a photograph of three American nuns out on a picnic. They were seated on a wharf in full habit, but one of them had removed her shoes and (*quel horreur!*) was publicly dangling her feet in the water. The shocked editor had printed above the photograph, "In America Anything Is Allowed!"

These examples are trivial in themselves, but they help to point up an important tension existing in American religious orders and congregations, a tension which must be resolved if American Catholic religious are to find the peace of soul and sense of personal fulfillment which is their right in their vocation.

Stated crudely, this tension may be described as arising from a mortal conflict between American spontaneity and practicality and medieval taboo. Note well, however, that the emphasis here is on the word "medieval." It would be a gross caricature of the situation religious face in this country were we to imagine chauvinistically that it is only American religious who are aware of the problems confronting religious orders and congregations in the twentieth century. There is today a tremendous ferment among the religious of other lands as well, a ferment full of the promise of immense spiritual growth in the years which lie ahead. Hence, in contrasting American spontaneity and medieval taboo I wish in no way to disparage the European religious spirit, which is manifesting a dynamic, creative thrust in many communities in Europe today. What I am referring to is its static historical residue in this country. For the fact of the matter is that the European religious who first transplanted their attitudes and institutions onto American soil were as thoroughgoingly European as the passengers on the *Mayflower*. Today, however, their Americanized successors find themselves with a fresh native spirit, cramped by the outmoded institutions of an ancient and now somewhat alien past.

American religious have a great deal to learn from a dialogue with their brethren from other lands. For it is only by the constant cross-fertilization of ideas that any group of people can hope to remain spiritually and religiously alive and vigorous. But a religious dialogue even within the Church presupposes genuine activity on both sides, and the religious thinking which we import from other lands must be critically evaluated and understood before it is accepted as relevant to the actual situation in this country.

Reflective American religious have long been so familiar with these tensions within their life that there would be no need for a book on the subject were it not that in the present generation things are building up to what could be a serious crisis. Vatican II indeed opened many Church windows that were for a long time sealed, and the winds have swept away many things that we had long thought were beyond question immovable. The coming generation of young religious has lots of questions to ask its predecessors. But they will not be content with catechism responses or snippets of some rule or custom book. The questions they are raising go much deeper than that, and so thoroughgoingly American are they that if they don't get real answers they are just apt to *do* something about it.

One important extrinsic factor which contributes considerably to the growing crisis is the emergence of the Catholic layman. It must be taken into account. In the past, the clerical or religious life seemed to be the only way open to religious-minded young people who wanted to dedicate themselves to the service of the Church. Nowadays this is far from the case. The new layman has already had considerable impact upon Church affairs, and as more and more Catholic laymen get into the swing of things this impact will certainly increase. As a result

29

the talented young religious or aspirant to the religious life often finds himself forced to face the nagging question of whether he might not actually serve the Church better as a layman than as a religious. With increasing frequency, he is asking himself, not whether he has the generosity to live the religious life, but whether a completely generous person will have a better opportunity to use his talents for Christ and his Church as a layman rather than as a religious. If there are any religious superiors left who think they can answer this question by quoting from the rule and the old ascetical manuals, or by applying the juridical yardstick of personal fidelity to external regulations, they are in for a rude awakening.

Another factor contributing to the growing anguish of young American religious is the present controversy over Catholic education. The backbone of the Catholic school system in this country is, of course, the religious orders. Moreover, it is by now completely apparent that some serious rethinking has got to take place concerning the purpose and function of Catholic education in America. Until that rethinking is done, and done scientifically and thoroughly, many young religious, whether rightly or wrongly, are going to remain haunted by the feeling that they have signed up on the crew of a sinking ship. To a talented young religious, for instance, the career of a Catholic lay professor on a secular campus is apt to seem much more a service of the interests of Christ and his Church than a life devoted to the preservation of a financially straitened, third-rate Catholic institution whose chances of having a significant impact upon the intellectual life of this country are practically nil. Superiors who have taught the young religious the meaning of indifference now find him calling into question (sometimes rashly and unjustly) their own indifference to the brick-and-mortar commitments of their orders. But in spite of his seeming rebelliousness the young religious is not afraid to serve the institutions of his order and to serve them generously. Still, in an age of accelerated cultural progress, his own personal and religious integrity forces him to demand that those institutions first seriously question and justify their right to exist in a changed and changing society.

Often, too, the younger generation of American religious are guilty of serious defects of human understanding and tactical blunders. They sometimes manifest a disconcerting willingness to throw out the baby with the bath, to ignore the solid achievements of their predecessors, dismissing with callous flippancy the often impressive results of decades of patient dedication, labor, and love. Naively oblivious of the limitations imposed by the concrete apostolic situation, they imagine themselves to be the only people in their orders who are conscious of the specific needs of the American Church, the only ones with enough vision to find the needed apostolic solutions. In a word, both the self-image of the young American religious and the stereotype which he tends to project

31

upon his predecessors are in frequent need of radical demythologizing.

But the lay movement and the crisis in education are in fact only ripples on the surface. The waters flow much deeper. They are, moreover, as American as the Mississippi and can no more be kept within the artificial structures that clutter much religious living than the Mississippi can be confined at flood tide.

One of the most striking contrasts between religious life as I have lived it in this country and in Europe is the value the European religious seems to place upon external ritual forms. Many European religious, at least as seen with American eyes, appear to have an almost insatiable appetite for elaborate public religious gestures and traditional, but impractical and outmoded, taboos. An example may help to illustrate what I mean. I once suggested to a mature Belgian religious that if the religious in his country would stop trying to identify with the poor by starving themselves and wearing patches on their habits and start trying to help the poor in a practical and permanent way to raise their standard of living, they might find the lower classes more impressed by the gospel message. Nonplussed by my blatantly materialistic approach to the preaching of the gospel, he replied, "But what about everything we learned in the novitiate?"

Let me say at once, however, that these remarks are in no way intended to underplay the importance of ritual in American Catholicism. In an age as liturgically conscious as our own, such a suggestion could hardly be tenable. But ritual is not the same thing as ritualism. There are, moreover, several legitimate approaches to the use of ritual, which vary according to circumstance and culture. In Europe, with its rich and ancient cultural heritage, the very pattern of life often assumes a spontaneously ritualistic tone; this is less evident in our "American way of life." One may argue that Americans are spiritually the poorer thereby. But be that as it may, such cultural deficiencies can be remedied only by the slow processes of national development. In the meantime, it is with the American mind as it exists that the American Church must deal; and it seems to me, at least, that the American spirit in its present state of development tends spontaneously to a ritual which is functionally integrated into the lives of our people and productive of some concrete religious result.

If such a functional approach to ritual seems to have its limitations, it does have certain advantages as well, as a brief reflection on the dangers of false ritualism will show. Carried to an extreme, the ritualistic cult of external forms for their own sake can easily degenerate into a kind of pharisaism. The "just" religious becomes the one who faithfully performs certain ritual acts which visibly symbolize his personal sanctity and dedication to God; the actions not included in this consecrated list become irreligious for him, and those who perform them secular-minded and unfit for the religious life. (As long as you

33

wear your phylactery where you know superiors can see it, you know that you will be all right.)

Another important consequence of a ritualistic approach to the religious life is the tendency, often unthematic or even subconscious, to exalt renunciation for its own sake as the goal of all religious living. Needless to say, religious life, like every other way of life, does involve renunciation. But when one's prevailing conception of religious living consists in the ritual performance of a series of impractical, symbolic acts, poverty, chastity, and obedience are themselves quickly transformed into a species of purely symbolic gesture in which the very facts of not possessing personal goods, of abstaining from married life, of submitting one's will to the will of another become the goal of one's personal religious striving and not a functional means of working with others toward a common apostolic purpose.

At its worst this cult of renunciation for its own sake degenerates into a Jansenistic suppression of "nature" that "grace" may more abound. For if holiness in a religious consists in renunciation, then obviously he is most holy who renounces most. So conceived, religious life can transform itself into a grotesque competition to see who can make himself most completely miserable in order to be the most completely pleasing to God. According to this logic, the total dedication of one's life to God in religion becomes the quest for that supreme moment of total human misery which constitutes true spiritual joy. This is, of course, a crude parody of the ideals of religious living; but where living has become the ritualistic cult of outmoded practices, the pursuit of even the loftiest ideals can hardly escape becoming a caricature of the reality.

The American spirit is at heart both experimentalist and functional. It is a forward-looking, gambling spirit willing to sacrifice almost anything for progress, for the hope of improvement. Our historical roots, though lengthening, are still too shallow in American soil for us to cling blindly to our past. As a result, in our bustling society there is little room for a spirituality of purely symbolic gesture. Our living is functional, and we need a spirituality that suits the way we live.

Nevertheless, the reader is apt to experience a twinge of legitimate concern at such a suggestion. It is sheer chauvinism to canonize everything about our "American way of life," and it is immense historical and theological folly to assume uncritically that everything about America is automatically compatible with the Christian message. Functional living in America, whatever its benefits in terms of our general standard of material prosperity, has produced some dreadfully depersonalizing results. It has fathered megalopolis with its swarming millions preoccupied with "not getting involved," whatever the price of our non-involvement might be to the other person. It has produced the cutthroat competition of Wall Street and Madison Avenue, the Organization Man, the bureaucratic cult of Unthink, our Babbits and our Main Streets.

Functional Asceticism

What possible place, then, can a functional approach to life find within a religious family founded, as it is, on selfless love? Even more, we are living in an age of personalism. Is not any effort to cope with human problems in terms of means and ends a regression into an essentialistic frame of reference with all the limitations that such a mentality implies?

These objections are important ones and must be taken seriously. But the difficulties they involve are not, I believe, insuperable. For although a functional spirit is, like all things human, subject to limitations and open to abuse, it has a legitimate place in the overall pattern of our life. And like any legitimate human aspiration, it can find its true fulfillment in the love of Christ.

Functional living need not be depersonalizing. The problem of ends and means is with us no matter how personal our ascetical viewpoint may become. It is a necessary moment within the moral situation. Moreover, the fundamental drive of a functional approach to life is precisely the conscious care to distinguish between what is an end and what is a means. Hence, if functional living is to be completely self-consistent, it must begin with a recognition that each human person, redeemed as he is by the love and grace of Christ, is morally speaking an end and can never be degraded to the level of a pure means. The failure of functionalism in this country is actually the failure of a truly functional spirit to be consistent with its own self-avowed principles.

Moreover, the functional asceticism I shall attempt to

describe in the pages which follow is not only functional but is also really an *asceticism*. As we shall see, it presupposes an apostolically-oriented community of selfless love as the matrix of its growth, and within such a community it consciously attempts to stimulate and mobilize the potential of each member for the effective accomplishment of the apostolic purpose which unites them all to one another in a living, personal bond of faith, hope, and love. Also, properly understood, functional asceticism can do much to preserve personalism from the sentimentality and relativism into which it easily degenerates.

Finally, I do not propose such an asceticism as the only possible ideal which a religious community may adopt. I suggest it merely as a legitimate ideal and as one which seems, to me at least, to be peculiarly suited to the spiritual needs of the religious men and women of this country.

For a long time now medieval ideals of ritualistic asceticism have survived alongside a nascent functional spirit in American religious orders. To thoughtful religious in the past, the combination must have seemed strange. But since, under the stress of the apostolate, few religious had the opportunity to reflect, many found little difficulty in bifurcating their minds by repeating the old ascetical formulas in theory while in practice the basic fabric of American religious life was slowly being rewoven to fit the pattern of an expanding technological society.

The spontaneous self-image of American religious

which has emerged from this process is radically different from its European archetype, although it is perhaps in many ways more profoundly Christian. What the religious of the new breed has learned from Vatican II is that this bifurcation of the mind is neither necessary nor desirable. His rebellion against phoniness and his quest for authenticity are in fact the expression of a need, grown suddenly thematic, to put an end to this division between theory and practice; to identify himself as what he is in fact and cannot, on this continent, in this nation and at this time, help being. For whereas the medieval religious tended to conceive of himself primarily as one who bears witness to Christ by publicly renouncing the good things of this world, the American religious conceives of himself primarily as involved in the immediate task of building the kingdom of God here on earth and as stripping himself for more efficiency in that enterprise by the triple renunciation of poverty, celibacy, and obedience.

Although at first glance these two ideals seem almost identical, they differ profoundly in the relative emphasis which they place upon different aspects of religious living and lead in practice to radically different approaches to the concrete details of religious life. Nevertheless, when translated into specifically functional terms, the ideal of involvement in the work of God's kingdom leaves ample room for heroic abnegation and self-sacrifice.

Let us take as a concrete example the matter of religious poverty. One reason why there is so much confusion in the minds of American religious as to the concrete meaning and witness value of religious poverty is that most religious have learned from their rules and ascetical manuals to think of poverty in absolute, univocal and abstract terms divorced from the apostolic work in which they are actually engaged. We learn in the manner of Cartesian rationalists to figure out apriori the "essence" of poverty and then in the manner of Roman jurists to impose this predefined ideal on everything we do.

By contrast, a functional approach to poverty would be fundamentally experimentalist: not renunciation for its own sake, but a renunciation proportioned to the concrete needs of the apostolic situation in which one finds oneself. It must be a renunciation for the sake of giving oneself to others more completely through apostolic work, the mode and degree of renunciation being determined by the concrete apostolic need and not by one's fidelity to a predetermined set of bureaucratic rules and regulations.

Far from being a relaxation of religious discipline, such an approach to poverty would demand far more of religious than the present practice of poverty. For one thing, it would place the burden of constantly re-evaluating the degree of one's self-renunciation in temporal matters squarely upon the consciences of individual religious and particular religious communities. It is all too easy, as matters now stand, to use the rules of one's order and the customs of common life to avoid ever feeling the pinch of actual poverty, while basking in the self-righteous sense of having always kept within the letter of the law.

Perhaps this last point needs further comment. Many

Functional Asceticism

American religious seem to find little difficulty in maintaining that their poverty is essentially a poverty of dependence upon superiors for proper permissions. Such an assertion is often, I believe, symptomatic of a mentality which I will attempt to describe in more detail in the following chapter. Here, however, we need only note the self-deception which can easily follow upon such an assumption. Taken to its logical conclusion, such a view of the meaning of poverty actually implies that the sanction of authority is sufficient to justify any expenditure, no matter how useless or sulf-indulgent it might be, viewed within the larger framework of the overall work and apostolic purpose of the order of which one is a member. Moreover, we need not look very far to find the origin of such a curious and potentially dangerous attitude. In most cases it has been carefully inculcated during the novitiate, when the young religious learned that he was living a "poor life" as long as he regularly asked permission for shoestrings and toothpaste. The transfer from such trivia to the spending of larger sums is spontaneous and, human nature being what it is, almost inevitable.

By contrast, a functional approach to poverty would not only demand more candor on the part of superiors as to the financial status of the communities they govern and the financial dimension of the apostolic opportunities open to the community, it would also demand of subjects the willingness to discuss openly with superiors the degree of personal renunciation which they as individual members of a community of apostolic endeavor would be willing to undertake in order to achieve their common apostolic goals more effectively.

Such a functional approach to poverty would presuppose, not abrogate, common life; and it would give it a meaning and an apostolic direction which it now almost totally lacks. The common life we practice at present is at best a symbolic gesture, at worst the securing by rote of trivial permissions and an empty ritualistic conformity to a set of bureaucratic house regulations. But in an American context, such a symbolic gesture is almost totally meaningless to religious themselves and almost totally valueless to non-religious as an act of public witness. On the other hand, a renunciation which would be visibly productive of concrete apostolic results is, in America at least, a renunciation with genuine religious meaning. To take just one banal example, superiors in this country who try to get their subjects to give up smoking as a symbolic gesture in the direction of poverty are foredoomed to disappointment. But should they propose to their subjects specifically a crying need in the apostolate which will go unfilled unless the money now spent for cigarettes is applied to it, I think they might be pleasantly surprised at the results.

Is it possible to approach religious chastity from a functional point of view? Many a religious may in fact experience a certain hesitation about attempting to do so. The vow of chastity is a deeply personal expression of his love

41

for God. Do we not actually risk degrading and depersonalizing it if we reduce it to nothing more than a means to an end? Isn't it possible that in approaching religious celibacy from a functional point of view we have reached ground too sacred to be trodden?

Perhaps; but I do not believe that an answer in the affirmative to these questions is inevitable. First of all, celibacy does indeed express in a striking way the love of a religious for God. But the Christian love of God is not simply identical with Christian celibacy. If, then, there is no necessary connection between the two, it follows that a Christian must have some reason for choosing celibacy as the expression of love of God which is best suited to him. To opt for a celibate life, for instance, because the consecration of one's virginity to God is more productive apostolically than the married state in no way degrades or depersonalizes the love which inspires such an option. But if an apostolically productive life is a good and legitimate reason for giving expression to one's love of God by a vow of celibacy, it follows that celibacy can and even should contribute something positive to one's total apostolic effectiveness, that celibacy as an expression of one's love for God has a functional role to perform in the total organization of one's life as a religious.

This conclusion is reinforced when a ritualistic approach to the meaning of religious celibacy and a functional approach are contrasted.

In matters of religious chastity, a ritualistic asceticism

tends to reduce the meaning of the vow to the moral "don'ts" of premarital chastity and a rigid adherence to the social taboos which have traditionally surrounded celibate life in common. As a result, it tends to be both negative and repressive.

A functional approach, on the other hand, would introduce a much healthier and more positive note into our understanding of the meaning of religious chastity. It would, for instance, recognize explicitly that the renunciation of marriage for the sake of the kingdom of Christ does not imply the renunciation of one's own sexuality. Unfortunately, in a society to which the idea has never occurred that a distinction can be made between sex itself and the adolescent ideal of sexual antics popularized in the media of mass entertainment, such a suggestion may seem, to some at least, just a bit shocking. But the distinction remains nevertheless real. For sexuality is far from being synonymous with sexual fulfillment in the physical sense. Sexuality is in its essence a particular way of existing as a person in human society. Hence, while marriage is a matter of choice, sexuality is not; and to renounce marriage for Christ and his kingdom in no way implies the renunciation of one's masculinity or femininity with whatever bearing it has on the way in which one orders one's life.

A functional approach to celibacy would, therefore, attempt to teach religious to integrate their mental and emotional endowments as man and woman with their

43

religious aspirations in such a way as to render their sexuality fruitful in their apostolic endeavors. It would, for instance, attempt to show the male religious that it is precisely his vow of celibacy which demands that he be a true and loving father to God's people in the same sense in which a Christian husband binds himself to be a true and loving father to his children. It would teach him that within the Christian community he must be a vital source of masculine decision, leadership, wisdom, and creativity. Similarly, a functional asceticism would teach the religious woman that she is to be the true and loving mother and sister to the brothers and sisters of Christ; and it would attempt to teach her how to integrate all of her instinctive feminine warmth, intuition, common sense, and dedication into a life of prayer and apostolic service.

Needless to say, there have been and are many religious men and women who have achieved and maintain emotional balance within the self-imposed restrictions of religious life. But it remains nevertheless true that they have on more than one occasion done so without, and even in spite of, the theoretical asceticism taught them in the course of their religious formation.

A functional approach to celibacy would, in other words, attempt to teach religious that human love is total, that ideally one cannot really love either God or one's neighbor with one's will alone, as opposed to one's emotions (even granting that the two are not identical faculties of the soul); that in order to be fully Christian, love for God

44

and for one's neighbor must arise from the whole of a man's concrete being. It would, in short, try to teach religious the basic scriptural message that true Christian love must proceed from the whole of a man's mind, from the whole of his strength, and from the whole of his *heart*—and hence, too, from the whole of his human affectivity. Thus it would present celibacy itself as one way of achieving genuine personal—and hence also sexual—maturity and fulfillment through the total dedication of one's sexed person to the service of God and of his kingdom. Religious chastity so conceived can, I believe, at least in an American context, take on a positive meaning and witness value transcending not only that of a purely ritualistic celibacy, with its emphasis on sexual repression and taboo, but also that of the negatively functional notion of a celibate life as purely a practical means of achieving a certain freedom of activity in the work of the apostolate.

Finally, and perhaps most important of all, a functional approach to the religious life would transform many of the current practices in the area of religious obedience. For where religious obedience is conceived as a fruitless symbolic gesture, submission of one's will to a superior is subtly transformed from a means into an end in itself. In truly functional obedience, on the other hand, submission to another can exist only for the sake of a common apostolic good to be achieved, and only to the extent that it is truly necessary to achieve that good. The witness value

45

of such a submission, as in the case of the other two
vows, would derive not from the fact that one deliberately
chooses something which is naturally repulsive (here, submission to another for its own sake) but from the fact
that the practical value of the apostolic goal in question
is one that can be grasped only in Christian faith and love.

What is important here is the frank and public recognition on the part of superiors that religious authority is
not an end in itself to be protected jealously by those
who wield it but a means of achieving a common apostolic purpose. More specifically, functional obedience
would mean that the questioning of a command, even
persistent questioning, on the part of the subject is not
insubordination as long as it is dictated by a mature and
conscientious concern for the apostolic interests of the
order. It would mean that a religious superior's commands
should be accepted by his subjects as what they are: not
as oracles from Olympus to be immediately and blindly
executed at all costs but as a human effort under grace
to reach a concretely shared apostolic objective, an effort
whose validity as law depends on the extent to which
it actually achieves the goal in question. A functional approach to obedience would mean that superiors would
apply existing regulations with a view to the personal
needs and apostolic capabilities of each individual subject, not enforce them blindly, rigidly, and to the letter.
It would mean that a superior's concern for the preservation of his religious institute would take the form of a

vital concern for the apostolic effectiveness of his community rather than for the ritual filling-out of a check-list of house regulations faithfully observed. It would mean that the exercise of authority is regarded not as the prerogative of a clerical aristocracy with special rights and privileges but as a necessary service to be performed within the group, for the sake of the group and of each individual member, and for the sake of their common apostolic goal. It would mean that dependence upon a superior must not reach the point at which it reduces the subject to a kind of infantilism in which he becomes incapable of making even the most elementary operational decisions, but must be decided, strictly and pragmatically, by the concrete needs of persons and situations, and not by the demands of an aprioristic "asceticism."

The older generation of American religious are becoming justifiably concerned for the new breed which they suddenly find so boisterously in their midst. It is my belief that those superiors who insist upon imposing outmoded ascetical patterns of religious living on the young aspirants to religious life in this country do indeed have cause for serious concern. But their concern should not be for the new breed. Whatever his faults (and they are real), the young religious's fierce preoccupation with personal religious integrity remains, I believe, one of the most palpable proofs of the stirring of the Spirit in American Catholicism. Their concern should rather be for themselves and for their orders. For a failure to understand the

47

aspirations of the younger generation and to adapt the forms of religious life to fit those aspirations means condemning religious orders and congregations in this country to be the dinosaurs of this revolutionary age. The inexorable penalty for the refusal to adapt has always been irrelevance, and the inevitable consequence of irrelevance in an age of accelerated change is ultimate extinction.

2 / NOMINALISM AND ASCETICISM

THE SUGGESTIONS of the previous chapter seem so obviously a matter of common sense that the very need to insist upon them poses a problem. Why is it that many American religious need to be reminded, and even convinced, of the functional nature of their own religious vows, even though it was precisely their personal dedication to the apostolic goals of their orders which led them to assume the obligation of the vows to begin with? Why this artificial dichotomy between the living religious aspiration and its formalized theoretical conceptualization?

A complete answer to these questions can be found only in a comprehensive history of religious orders in this country. Needless to say, such a history is far beyond the scope of this book, and it is also beyond the competence of its author. I would like, however, in the pages which follow, to attempt to highlight what seems to me to be an important speculative aspect of the problem. In so doing I in no way wish to underestimate the importance of the historical, sociological, psychological, and other factors which no doubt have been and are both operative and important in the development of American religious asceticism. But I do wish to suggest that the intellectual factor of which I shall speak has been of tremendous importance in influencing our total approach to those same historical, sociological, psychological, and other factors.

More specifically, I would like to suggest that many of the concrete ascetical practices and attitudes prevalent in religious orders in this country are the result of a particular way (or method) of thinking about religious problems. This method of religious thinking is only one of many possible ways of going about the business of theologizing; it is subject to real limitations; and unless these limitations are critically reflected upon and transcended they will not only seriously cripple the work of dogmatic and moral theology but will lead inevitably to the fossilization of asceticism in irrelevant ritualistic forms and practices. The mode of thinking to which I refer can perhaps best be characterized as a species of theological nominalism. The asceticism which stems from it and corresponds to it I shall call "ascetical nominalism."

Nominalism is not restricted to religious thinking. It is found in all forms of human thought, and hence almost seems to result from some innate defect in the human mind. Since, then, theological nominalism is only one of the many possible forms which nominalism can take, I shall first attempt to describe the generic nature of nominalism as such and then proceed to a consideration of the major characteristics of its specifically theological manifestation.

52

Men think about the things they experience. There are, then, in the conceptualization of reality three fundamental elements which should be distinguished: the reality itself, my experience of the reality, and my verbal conceptualization of that experience. For while there is a certain structure of content common to the reality, my experience of it, and my conceptualization of that experience, the three are far from being simply congruent and identical. My experience is always a *partial* awareness of the total structure of the reality itself; and my concepts always exclude the greater part of my experience from their specific content. Hence, just as the conceptual verbalization of my experience is only a very partial expression of the whole of my experience, so the whole of my experience is only a partial awareness of the total structure of the realities which act upon my consciousness. A nominalist is a person who makes the mistake, disastrous in the speculative sphere, of identifying the realities of experience with its verbal articulation (and, in the case of a thoroughgoing nominalism, with a particular verbal articulation).

The theological nominalist is one who commits the same blunder with regard to the truths of revelation. That is to say, he spontaneously substitutes for the events of salvation themselves one particular verbal formulation of belief.

It is not my intention, in the remarks which follow, to pass judgment upon the theological nominalist. Theological nominalism is part of our common religious heritage; we have all benefited from it as well as, in some measure, fallen victim to its intrinsic limits. Nor is it my intention here to reject utterly a tradition which has made some solid contributions to the growth and progress of the Church in this country. Complete repudiation of any movement of thought inevitably results in a repudiation of those legitimate human values which the movement itself sought to preserve. We do not so much need to repudiate our nominalistic heritage as to reflect upon its limitations and, transcending them, to reincorporate what is truly valid in the nominalistic viewpoint into a larger frame of theological reference. The process is one of growth, not of rejection; and it should in no way be interpreted as a threat to any of the solid accomplishments of the past.

The historical origins of theological nominalism are interesting to study. The research of Professor Gilson has in particular helped to throw considerable light upon its beginnings. As Gilson points out in his *History of Christian Philosophy in the Middle Ages,* the condemnation of Latin Averroism by Etienne Tempier, Bishop of Paris, in 1270 only served to accelerate the growth of a distrust of human reason that was beginning to emerge in scholastic theological circles. Driven to its logical conclusion, this distrust led ultimately to the almost total banishment of philosophical reflection from the theological sanctuary and the emergence of what came to be known as positive theology. (Significantly enough, it is often positive theology in one form or another which is still being taught in today's seminaries.)

Convinced of the unreliability of the human mind in matters of divine revelation, the positive theologian began to search for some certain haven of speculative security. He found it finally in an uncompromising adherence to Sacred Scripture and the authority of the Church as the only sure rule of orthodox belief. Increasingly distrustful of his own ability to reach theological truth by rational reflection, he thus gradually transformed "proof" in theology into the search for officially sanctioned texts in the sources of revelation which would support (preferably with the exact same verbal expressions for the sake of greater security) a given theological thesis. The role of reason was thus strictly subordinated to textual analysis, rational reflection in theology having now no other purpose than to manifest the absence of contradiction between the documentary sources of revelation and human experience.

Whatever his faults, the positive theologian had hold of a genuine theological truth. Revelation is not deducible from the first principles of human reason; nor can the supernatural *as supernatural* be grasped by the natural powers of man (although one cannot conclude from this fact alone, as Karl Rahner and others have recently been at pains to point out, that grace has no impact whatever upon human consciousness). But in disparaging man's ability to reach truth by his natural reason, the positive theologians were in fact sowing the wind. The whirlwind came with the Protestant Reformation.

One of Luther's great gifts was his ability to play off both ends of positive theology against the middle. Combining a theory of the inner corruption of man's mind and will with a nominalistic notion of imputed justification, he sought to vindicate his position by pitting the two great authorities of positive theology, Scripture and Tradition, against one another. By casting his lot with Scripture, he provoked an exaggerated response in Catholic theological circles in the direction of Tradition. As a result, with the institutionalization of clerical training which followed upon Trent, Luther unwittingly fixed the pattern of clerical (and through it, of religious and lay) instruction which, with minor variations, has been in force from that day to this.

The concrete impact of these historical events upon the thought patterns of the Church can perhaps be best illustrated by considering the plight of a hypothetical seminarian seeking intellectual and spiritual formation in a hypothetical seminary where nominalism is the order of the day.

We prescind here completely from the problem of whether such seminaries actually exist today or not. Given the historical laws of the gradual transformation of institutions, however, the real problem probably concerns the degree to which they still exist. Fortunately, seminary reform in this country has shown heartening progress in the past few years, but no one can deny that much still remains to be done.

But to return to the point: What, concretely, might await our purely hypothetical seminarian about to embark upon a hypothetical theological career in a hypothetical seminary of, let us say, the rigidly nominalistic nineteenth-century variety? What sort of intellectual and disciplinary formation is he likely to encounter?

It is only fair to warn the reader that the remarks which follow constitute something of a caricature. But though this method will suffer from all the basic limitations of a caricature—most notably, distortion through oversimplification—we hope it will also involve some of the advantages of caricature. For by a certain amount of oversimplification we may be able to present in sharper focus some of the key facets of a significant religious mentality.

If, then, our hypothetical seminarian is a typical seminarian, he has from the beginning of his training been taught to look forward to the study of theology as the queen of the sciences. If, however, he is in addition a-typically thoughtful, the shock of discovering, on his arrival at a theologate, that the summit of human reflection on the truths of revelation is reached in what is only a jaded and thinly disguised species of nominalism might occasion a terrible disillusionment, or even a crisis of faith.

But fortunately (or unfortunately) the typical American seminarian has rarely been as thoughtful as that. Still, expecting to find the living word of God in theology, our hypothetical seminarian encounters instead a list of Denzinger numbers and a loose catalogue of Scripture texts, disjointed and half-understood. He discovers that "scientific theology" can only mean by definition what remains of revealed truth once it has been squeezed through the fine strainer of the entrenched theological methodology. He learns that "proof" in theology is conceived as quantitative, a kind of nose-counting which results in the accumulation of the maximum number of approved authorities who have said the same thing as some textbook thesis. He learns that reflection is not really of first importance in theology, because each thesis expresses a mystery, and in matters of mystery one should be satisfied with repeating the divinely approved formulas sanctioned by Scripture and Tradition. He learns that the vocabulary in theology is a closed circle, and that its proper use is confined to those already initiated into the mysteries of the entrenched methodology. He infers that theology is relatively easy to master after all, that if one can only memorize sufficiently well the thesis definitions, plus the corresponding Scripture quotes and Denzinger numbers, one can get through the whole of theology without having had to perform a single act of critical reflection. Worst of all, he learns all these things not so much by being *taught them explicitly in class* as by *absorbing them unconsciously* through constant immersion in a *way of thinking* that is at heart nominalistic.

58

Now it is precisely because he absorbs these attitudes implicitly, by a kind of pedagogical osmosis, that theological nominalism can become a kind of spiritual sickness with which he is afflicted rather than one speculative school of thought, among others, in which he is trained. For as long as the basic methodological presuppositions of theological nominalism remain operative unthematically in one's religious thinking, one will inevitably be their intellectual prisoner. We are all, of course, to some extent the victims of our own methodological presuppositions. But unfortunately for our hypothetical seminarian, the consequences of unexamined nominalistic presuppositions both for himself and for those charged with his education can prove particularly disastrous.

Owing to the ecclesiastical legislation which followed upon Trent, some degree of intellectual inbreeding has become unavoidable in seminary training. The faculty and administrators of any seminary are themselves former seminarians, most of them products of the seminary they now administer and instruct. Most of them are, moreover, graduates of a Roman university whose intellectual contact with the non-clerical world barely exceeds what they encountered in their initial seminary training. Add to this inbreeding a rigidly nominalistic cast of thought, and the result is what has come to be called in modern times a "ghetto seminary."

The distinguishing characteristics of the typical ghetto seminary are worth noting. The first is a conscious quest for intellectual isolation. This deliberate policy is perhaps the most spontaneous reaction of an out-and-out theological nominalism in the face of an intellectually pluralistic society. For having relegated the use of reason to the outer fringes of theology, the nominalist finds himself intellectually naked before the attacks of those who not only refuse to follow his example but even (think of it!) refuse to cower when he begins to wave the mace of ecclesiastical authority. Further, the true nominalist is more often than not at a loss even to grasp the point of the attacks which so dismay him. Having reduced the whole of religious truth to a closed set of categories, he finds it impossible to talk about revelation with anyone who does not employ these same approved terms. Indeed, he spontaneously tends to attribute their use of "alien" thought patterns either to their stiff-necked refusal to respect divine authority or to their failure to grasp the full beauty of his position. Never having questioned his own methodological presuppositions, he does not suspect that part of the difficulty may lie with himself and his particular approach to the articulation of religious truth. Being thus ill equipped to refute the statements of the *adversarii*, or even to understand their difficulties, the teachers and administrators of our hypothetical nominalistic seminary find what comfort they can in preserving the seminarians entrusted to their care from the contamination which comes from contact with the evil powers lying outside the protective circle of words they have drawn around them. In seeking to isolate seminarians from the modern world, the nominalist is, then, acting, as far as he can judge objectively, for their own good. And for that very reason, his pain and chagrin at discovering the bitter resentment these same seminarians may feel at this "protective" isolation is sincere and heartfelt. In the limited world in which the theological nominalist lives, such rebellion can only bear the name of blind ingratitude.

The rigid regimentation which is the second characteristic of the ghetto seminary is, in part at least, another product of the nominalistic mentality. Being a way of thinking more than a set of propositions, theological nominalism is able to permeate religious thought and action. In moral theology, it has given rise to the excessive legalism which characterizes so much of Catholic moral thinking. For just as the nominalistic dogmatist can find no speculative certitude except in the approved formulas of official professions of faith, so the nominalistic moralist can find no sound basis for moral choice except in those norms of conduct officially approved by Church authority. The result is a Christian ethics which is legalistic, aprioristic, and deductive and (be it noted) a Christian asceticism based almost exclusively upon blind assent to religious authority as the only "sure" path to holiness.

Hence, any deviation among seminarians from the pattern set by the rules and regulations of the ghetto seminary is apt to be interpreted by superiors as a dangerous sign of their personal rebellion against the express and juridically correct will of God. In other words, just as the

61

nominalistic dogmatist's presuppositions force him to detach rational understanding as much as possible from speculative religious assent, so too in the practical sphere they lead to the separation of rules and laws from the functional purpose which led to their original formulation. A rule must be observed not because it is an effective means of reaching a specific end but simply because it is sanctioned by authority (and hence, to the unreflective nominalist, whether it achieves the purpose for which it is formulated or not).

Bureaucratic suspicion on the part of seminary authorities toward any changes which do not originate from higher up in the bureaucracy is the third characteristic of the ghetto seminary. This phenomenon becomes much more intelligible from the viewpoint of a thoroughgoing nominalistic legalism. Having reduced religious assent uncritically to his own nominalistic definition of religious assent, the administrator of the ghetto seminary finds himself automatically suspicious of any movement of thought or opinion which does not bear from the first the juridical sanction of Church officialdom. The prophetic role of the Christian within the Church which at present consists basically in the effort to sort out the tangle of means and ends that excessive legalism has brought the Church to, is unintelligible in a nominalistic universe. Indeed, the very sincerity of the nominalist's theological convictions makes what seems like the rebellion of the younger generation against the order established by God as great a source of anguish for him as his intransigence is to his charges.

Finally, where nominalism is the prevailing intellectual mood, the inevitable result is speculative authoritarianism and sterility. Had theological nominalism been able to exist in a vacuum, it would have remained innocuous enough. But, in its Catholic version at least, it is ordinarily accompanied by a number of attitudes which render it potentially very dangerous. It is, perhaps, at its most dangerous when it is accompanied by a sincere religious zeal. For, having traded the events of salvation for a closed set of theological concepts, the truly zealous nominalist feels *conscience-bound* to make every other man into his own theological image. Commitment to Christ becomes for him exclusive commitment to a fixed set of approved theological formulas. The speculative elaboration of revelation, where it is attempted at all, becomes strictly limited to those philosophical terms and concepts which have already received official and long-standing Church approbation. Originality being, by definition, unsanctioned is automatically suspect; and "safe" scholarship becomes limited to textual studies of approved authors.

I have been speaking of the intellectual and disciplinary formation given to a hypothetical seminarian in a hypothetical seminary in which a rigid nominalism is the prevailing atmosphere. My purpose in so doing, let me repeat, has not been to describe any existing institution, although clerical and religious readers of these lines may encounter from time to time a pattern of thought and action familiar from their own training. My specific purpose in drawing this hypothetical portrait in some detail should become clearer as we proceed. Here, however, it is important to note that those among the clergy and religious who have succumbed to the distorting effects of a nominalistic formation remain to a great extent the passive victims of their own training. They are fundamentally good people. Many of them are probably saintly people. Their personal sincerity and profound devotion to the Church remain beyond question. Indeed, often enough it is their very nominalistic cast of thought which leads them to make heroic personal sacrifices for the sake of their faith. Often, pathetically, being unable even to understand the dehumanizing effects of their speculative training, to say nothing of approving them, they are at a loss to know what remedy to apply.

The plight of the sincerely distressed nominalist helps to accentuate a number of important facets of the nominalistic mind. For we would do the nominalist a serious injustice were we to think of him as a simple soul. In point of fact his complexity can at times make him appear to the passive observer to be a walking set of contradictions.

He is, for instance, a strange mixture of profound humility and intellectual arrogance. In his unquestioning submission to the teaching authority of the Church, he manifests a degree of devotion which is unselfish and heroically self-abasing. At the same time, his identification of the whole of revealed truth with a closed set of verbal formulas makes him haughtily intolerant of any attempt to reformulate the message of salvation in the language of contemporary men. This haughtiness not only embraces those outside the Church whose thinking is for him by definition anathema; it can even extend to members of his own faith whose "imprudent" zeal to communicate the momentous events of salvation to other men leads them to stray from the "tried and true" formulas of traditional theology.

Similarly, although he may be burning with zeal for the spread of Christ's message, he remains completely unconscious of the fact that his particular formulation of that message is irrelevant to the intellectual climate of the society in which he lives.

Caught in his own methodological presuppositions, he cannot distinguish between questioning the truth of a statement and questioning the relevance of its concrete verbal formulation in a given situation. As a result, his nominalism will automatically lend a rationalistic quality to all of his thinking. Convinced that his only certitude lies in the documents of revelation, and apprehensive of any personal reflection upon the actual meaning of those documents, he must somehow try to fit the whole of human religious experience into the limited number of theological categories thus placed at his command. When those categories prove inadequate for his speculative needs he characteristically appeals to some inscrutable divine decree that things be just as he has explained them, in spite of the fact that he himself recognizes the inadequacy of his own position, from the speculative point of view.

At this point, the reader is probably tempted to say to himself, "This is all very well, but what has it got to do with the problem of this book?" The question is a good one; for what the reader is really asking is: What is the precise relationship between dogmatic and moral nominalism and its ascetical counterpart?

Speculative nominalism—both dogmatic and moral—is, as we have seen, an attempt to substitute for the persons and events of salvation a particular set of officially sanctioned formulas and abstract principles of conduct. By the same token, ascetical nominalism is the rigidly formalistic attempt to substitute a particular set of sanctioned rules and pious practices for the all-important religious event of personal sanctification and for the gradual and vital assimilation of each individual Christian as an individual to the message and saving grace of Christ. It is in effect the effort to define the meaning of sanctity theoretically, abstractly, and apriori by appeal to approved ascetical formulas and to impose that definition rigidly and absolutely upon the personal lives of each individual Christian, regardless of his personal, individual needs and concrete situation.

Given the tendency of all popular manifestations of piety to degenerate into superstition and taboo, one would be hard put to it to attribute all the ascetical ills of the Church to nominalism alone. At the same time, there can be little doubt that the two tendencies have interacted. For ascetical nominalism pursued uncritically can give a sophistication and a kind of abstract justification to the perpetuation of practices based on formalism and taboo by seeming to lend them the weight of an absolute authority.

But be that as it may, ascetical nominalism, where it does exist, can be detected by a series of symptoms which closely parallel those of speculative nominalism noted above. Thus, just as speculative nominalism leads to a deliberate policy of intellectual isolation and to the protective withdrawal of the Church from any contaminating contact with the world of profane and secular thought, so too ascetical nominalism leads inevitably to a rigid and artificial distinction between a life which is "religious" and dedicated to the ritual performance of certain specified holy actions and one which is "secular" and "profane." In making such a distinction, the nominalist is consistent with his own principles. For adhering to authority as the only norm of certitude, he must as a result inevitably conclude that the only sure path to God, the only certain norm of holiness, must be those practices and customs which bear the stamp of official approval. Now, unfortunately, the tragic consequence of conceiving only certain sanctioned practices as certainly holy and religious is that one inevitably comes to regard all other actions, even

67

good, legitimate human ones, as being at best suspect and at worst positively "secular." The "unsanctioned" becomes equated with the "tainted," and the process of holiness becomes identified with the systematic withdrawal from anything which does not bear the purifying blessing of authority.

The legalism of a purely deductive moral theology which is the hallmark of speculative nominalism is translated at the ascetical level into a spirituality based almost exclusively upon external observance. Fidelity to prayer becomes transformed into unfailing presence in one's room during the time of meditation and regular attendance in chapel during prescribed common exercises. Mortification becomes the faithful performance of certain traditional penances. External regularity becomes the only sure norm of "true holiness" and adherence by rote to external discipline the only certain mark of a "good religious."

Along with this ascetical legalism there comes inevitably the bureaucratic stifling of creativity, initiative, and imagination in the spiritual life. Each religious is presented with a predefined and officially approved image of himself and trained to conform his life carefully to it if he wishes to find God. Individual movements of the heart which fail to conform to the approved pattern become automatically suspect, tell-tale indications of deep-rooted spiritual pride and of a lack of inner docility and submission to God's will.

Finally, the intellectual sterility of speculative nominalism finds its counterpart in the spiritual sterility of the nominalistic ascetic. Having traded the love of Christ for the rigid observance of the law, and the fullness of Christian living for routine fidelity to a predefined list of approved "religious" actions, the ascetical nominalist turns himself into a New Testament version of the Pharisee: self-righteous in his sanctity, intolerant of the deviations of others, bent in conscience upon transforming everyone else into his own ascetical image, a strange combination of spiritual humility and spiritual pride, vaguely sensing the emptiness of his life, but bearing it all (God help us) "in union with Christ"—a caricature of holiness, and at heart a human and a religious failure.

To a large extent, though not exclusively, the problem of aggiornamento in this country is the problem of learning to cope with our nineteenth- and early twentieth-century nominalistic heritage. It is a heritage still very much alive in its contemporary consequences, and we still have a long way to go before we can store it away in our museum of historical curiosities.

Nevertheless, any genuine renewal must begin by a frank recognition of nominalism's positive contributions to the American Catholic tradition. They are far from negligible. To begin with, Catholics in this country, living as they do in an atmosphere of religious fragmentation and sometimes even secular hostility, desperately need some clear norm of spiritual self-identity. By its constant insistence on the teaching authority of the Church, nominalism provided that norm. The magisterium of the Church, always an essential element of Catholic belief, became under the nominalist's insistence the rock of truth in a religious sea tossed by the storm winds of error and strife. Even a brief glance at the doctrinal fragmentation of contemporary American Protestantism will give some insight into the importance of this accomplishment.

In addition, even though nominalism represents only one of many possible theological schools of thought, it seems to highlight a number of important dogmatic truths—not the least of these being that any attempt to formulate the events of salvation in conceptual terms must ultimately dissolve in mystery. It has established clearly the rights of the teaching authority of the Church in matters of faith and morals (not so clearly, however, that there is now no room for further reflection). It has underscored the basic dogmatic fact that in the last analysis the certitude of faith is not based upon rational deduction but upon the fidelity of God revealing himself to us in his incarnate Word. Finally, it has brought theologians to a much more explicit consciousness of the need for thorough research into the documentary sources of revelation and has led them to a real awareness of the word as an integral element within the self-revelation of God to man.

Under enlightened Church leadership, the work of postconciliar reconstruction is already well under way in

70

many seminaries and religious orders and congregations. But this work will never be ultimately effective unless it is carried on in a spirit of genuine experimentation by the ongoing and mutually corrective interaction of theory and practice. For unfortunately "renewal" itself can often be a weasel word; and for a thoroughgoing nominalist who is nevertheless open to the possibility of change, "renewal" is all too apt to mean the apriori construction of a new set of abstract speculative and practical notions and directives capable of being enacted bureaucratically into a universal law binding upon all and imposed willy-nilly upon every concrete situation whether it is relevant or not. The nominalistic version of renewal consists, in other words, not in changing one's attitude toward law but in changing from one legal straitjacket to another. But true renewal is and must always be a constant process. It is essentially experimental in spirit, the vital effort constantly to re-evaluate and to re-adapt to the ever changing situation both speculatively and practically. We do not need just changes; we need a structural apparatus to make change an ever present possibility.

At a speculative level we can make good use of much of the work that has already been done by the creative theological minds of this generation. To cite only one obvious example, Karl Rahner's contributions to the theological aggiornamento are of outstanding significance. His Christology, his theology of nature and grace, his repudiation under hints from de Lubac of existential "extrinsicism" in explaining the supernatural, his insistence that no theology is terminal and that each generation must rethink, in terms meaningful to itself, the sense of the divine message of salvation—all these factors in Rahner's thought have already given speculative theology a healthy thrust beyond the limitations of a purely nominalistic methodology. But Rahner is only one of many such theologians. In this country, the efforts of men like Frs. Cooke, Courtney Murray and McKenzie, among others, are already too well known to need further attention.

But the process of speculative renovation must be accompanied by important revisions in the practical running of American seminaries and religious houses, particularly religious houses of formation, both in the organization of their curriculum and in matters of external discipline. For just as many of the speculative conclusions of nominalism are the product of a particular way of going about theology rather than of any explicitly formulated premises, so too revision in the concrete way of going about the task of theologizing and of regulating the daily life of a clerical or religious community is bound to have salutary effects finally in the speculative sphere as well.

At the level of speculative reform, the following changes would, I believe, be worth attempting. These are, however, only suggestions, needing to be tested experimentally.

First of all, it is evident that we do need some sort of revision of the courses offered in theologates both for secular clergy and for religious. The present thesis-discipline method of presentation is not only intellectually stifling, it is also pedagogically cumbersome. It is possible, for instance, under the present system for a seminarian to spend more than two semesters of class time reviewing the utterly dead and irrelevant controversy over efficacious and sufficient grace for the simple reason that, as a result of the artificial dissection of philosophy from theology and of theology itself into special disciplines, exactly the same matter must be treated in three separate courses.

Instead of an artificial and outmoded thesis-discipline approach to theology, the achievements of Christian reflection upon the truths of revelation should be studied in a fully historical context. Instead of an arbitrary systematization of the matter of theology (in which, for instance, the one God must be considered separately from the triune God), the events of salvation history themselves might provide a much better basis for the speculative organization of course material in dogma. The seminarian could be made to follow the gradual evolution of theological thinking from the Old and New Testaments right down to contemporary theological reflections. This historical survey of the development of dogma might occupy the first two years of his theological training. The first year would be devoted exclusively to the study of

Scripture with special emphasis upon those passages which will serve as the basis of subsequent theological development. Second year would be devoted to a historical survey of the major theological controversies in the history of the Church, with special care being given to the historical interpretation of key conciliar texts through a more systematic application to Church documents of the methods of modern scriptural exegesis. Minor courses like Church history and patrology could simply be absorbed into this historical survey of dogmatic development instead of cluttering the daily schedule with necessarily superficial lectures.

The third year of theology (and where it exists, the fourth) could then be spent in the explicit speculative confrontation of the teaching of Scripture and of the Church with the concrete needs of modern men living in contemporary society, among whom, by the way, we must number the student of theology himself. In this third and fourth year of training especially, the greatest latitude should be given to students to prepare themselves individually for the specific kind of work they will be engaged in later on.

The basic drive of this final phase of theology would be the translation of the message of Christ into terms comprehensible to contemporary man. There is no reason, of course, why this process of translation cannot be begun in the first two "historical" years of theological training. At this final stage, current theological controversies, catechetics, homiletics, and liturgy would be studied in detail. By thus approaching dogmatic theology within a fully historical context and consciously attempting to focus the riches of Catholic tradition upon his contemporary situation, the student will learn to think of theology as the thing that it is—namely, a vital growing process rather than the static codification of half-understood ecclesiastical documents.

By the same token a more historical approach to canon law and official statements of the Church in moral matters might do much to eliminate the nominalistic legalism that encumbers large areas of moral theology. The very practical orientation of moral theology, in this country at least, has helped to preserve it from the degree of irrelevance that has characterized much of our dogmatic thinking. Yet even in moral theology much remains to be done.

These curriculum revisions in theological training would, I believe, need to be supplemented by revisions in philosophical training as well. Thus, as the approach to theology becomes more historical, the philosophical training of seminarians and religious would inevitably be brought into line. For whether they are willing to admit it or not, philosophate teachers and administrators often labor under much the same sort of nominalistic bias as their theologate colleagues. Even should experimentation show, as I suspect it will, that some sort of systematic metaphysical training is still necessary, the present curriculum of formal philosophical disciplines can stand considerable telescoping and radical rethinking.

Here again, however, the training of seminarians and religious should be focused primarily upon the contemporary philosophical situation, whose modes of thought they must understand thoroughly if they are to make the message of salvation relevant in them. As in theology, the philosophy course should be so organized that philosophy itself appears to be a vital reflective process rather than a rigid catechism of stock responses to stock questions. Accordingly, the first year of philosophy would probably be best spent in a fairly comprehensive survey of the development of philosophical thought, and the rest of philosophy in a study of some sort of systematic metaphysics and of those questions which most preoccupy contemporary philosophical thinkers. American philosophy should receive special attention.

The humanistic formation of seminarians and religious should also be made to keep pace with philosophy and theology. Although acquaintance with the classics of Greek and Roman literature is necessary for a well-rounded education, they can hardly provide the hard core of a relevant literary formation. Classical training can be accomplished nowadays mainly in translation and in private readings followed by discussion. More extensive training in Latin might be provided for those destined for advance studies in either philosophy or theology. Much more emphasis should be given to modern languages. In literature much more emphasis should be given to the development of American literature and to the study of contemporary literary movements and criticism.

The path toward disciplinary reform has already been pointed out by Cardinal Ritter, who recently liberalized the regulations governing his St. Louis seminarians. The basic drive in such disciplinary reform should be to force the individual seminarian or religious to assume much more personal responsibility for his actions and to encourage responsible initiative and personal creativity to the greatest possible extent. Seminarians and religious still in the process of formation must be made to see that becoming a priest or a religious does not mean being forced into a predetermined juridical mould, that the enterprise is truly one of creative exploration into God.

But theological renewal will not be complete unless dogmatic, moral, philosophical, and disciplinary reforms are accompanied by a thoroughgoing ascetical renewal. And, just as dogmatic and moral renewal must begin by acknowledging the contributions of the nominalistic tradition in order to preserve whatever is of positive value in it while expanding its methodological frame of reference, so too ascetical renewal must begin by acknowledging the positive insights of ascetical nominalism and then, by correcting its limitations, proceed to the task of rethinking ascetical values in an enlarged conceptual frame of reference.

The great contribution of ascetical nominalism is its insistence upon the importance of authority as a concrete revelation of the will of God. No genuine asceticism can ever gainsay the basic validity of that insight. The flaw in ascetical nominalism, however, is its attempt to dissociate the binding force of authority from the end for which it was originally established and thus to convert what was originally a means into an end in itself.

Functional asceticism would, by contrast, seek to restore to religious authority an explicit recognition of its essentially constitutive purpose, and by so doing to involve it in a continuing and fruitful dialogue with critical reflection which will ultimately enable it to accomplish even more perfectly its divinely established mission.

A brief consideration of some of the concrete consequences of such a reorientation of asceticism will provide the basic theme of the chapters which follow.

But before we begin these further reflections, it is, perhaps, important to remind the reader once again of the scope and limitations of the foregoing remarks. These reflections are not intended to be a complete and adequate diagnosis of the whole problem of religious renewal in this country but only of what seems to me to be one important speculative aspect of the problem. It would also be grossly unjust on the basis of these few remarks to seek to cast every superior in the role of a nominalistic Simon Legree. Often enough superiors are deeply conscious of the need for change and deeply concerned by their temporary inability to meet that need. Often, too, the very effort to meet the most immediate and obvious needs of their subjects leaves them little time for the more general reforms they would wish to effect. Our thinking in such matters is already too much plagued with artificial and somewhat bigoted stereotypes to add that of "nominalist" to the list.

3 / A FUNCTIONAL APPROACH TO ASCETICAL RENEWAL

It should by now be clear that a functional approach to asceticism would provide a useful method for re-evaluating many of the practices of ascetical nominalism. It could, for instance, transform at a concrete interpersonal level the relationship that exists between superior and subject.

In a nominalistic framework any personal relationship between the two is at best difficult, at worst impossible; and where it is possible, it is likely to degenerate into an outdated religious paternalism (or maternalism, as the case may be). For, however kind a superior may be personally, if he conceives of and actually uses his authority nominalistically, there is ultimately nothing to mediate between his will and that of his subject. The two wills stand not only in potential opposition to one another but in an opposition which is very much like the confrontation of two alien brute forces.

For the overriding concern of the truly nominalistic superior is to play things strictly according to the book, to enforce impartially and without regard to persons the divinely sanctioned rules and customs of his order. He stands before his subjects, therefore, not so much as a person like themselves but rather as the concrete embodiment of an absolute divine will to which they must unquestioningly bend their own wills and even intellects or stray from the sure path of perfection.

Needless to say, in such a view of religious authority, any genuinely personal relationship with one's superiors becomes foredoomed. When a superior is conceived as nothing more than the human embodiment of an ultimately unquestionable absolute, no subject can truly regard him as a friend, a brother—nor, indeed, as another human being like himself, with human hopes, fears, frustrations, and aspirations.

A functional asceticism would, I believe, eliminate this element of impersonality from our conception of the superior-subject relationship while preserving the proper subordination of the one to the authority of the other. For in a functional context, the authority of the superior appears, not as a species of extrinsic divine sanction which automatically transforms his will into the objective norm of his subject's perfection, but rather as a necessary and providential means whereby superior and subject are enabled to co-ordinate their efforts in pursuit of a concrete apostolic end to which they commonly aspire. Then the only absolute is the end itself; the authority which finds expression in the deliberated decisions of the superior's will remains, together with those decisions, only a means to that end, and hence necessarily relative to it and judged and measured by its scope.

Hence, in a functional context, for a subject to acknowledge the authority of his superior is in the first instance for him to acknowledge the personal aspiration to a common apostolic goal which binds them together. His submission thus becomes the functionally necessary but freely accepted subordination of one person to another for the sake of a common enterprise (in this case, one intelligible only in the light of faith), whose accomplishment depends concretely on the co-operative search of both superior and subject for the best means to bring their labors to fulfillment.

In other words, functional asceticism would force both superior and subject to begin their relationship with a frank mutual admission of their human fallibility and would add to this an insistence upon the need they have for one another in order to reach the supernatural goal to which they both freely aspire. Fully comprehended, such a relationship would not only be apostolically fruitful but deeply personal as well.

A functional approach would also help superior-subject relations to avoid some of the dangerous and depersonalizing blunders of those younger and less reflective members of the new breed who, in repudiating a nominalistic notion of authority-for-its-own-sake, run to the opposite extreme of conceiving authority as existing exclusively for the sake of their own personal self-fulfillment.

The problem of self-fulfillment in religion is an important one, and we shall return to it in a somewhat different context in the following chapter. Here we need only note that the error of absolutizing the self-fulfillment of the subject and completely subordinating the will and authority of the superior to it is as ultimately depersonalizing as the opposite one of absolutizing every decision which proceeds from those in authority. In the latter case it is the superior who attempts to reduce the subject to the status of an impersonal instrument for the fulfillment of the letter of the law; in the former it is the subject who attempts to reduce the superior to the status of an impersonal tool of his own individual growth and personal self-development.

Thus we occasionally find some thoughtless young religious bitterly complaining of superiors who stunt the personal growth of their subjects by failing to treat them as persons and individuals, while they themselves do not hesitate to assume an utterly calloused attitude toward those same superiors and to display in their mutual dealings a total disregard for the superior's own feelings and personal needs.

A functional approach to asceticism would obviate this particular difficulty by making it clear from the start that in a religious community superiors do not exist exclusively for the sake of their subjects, any more than subjects do for the sake of superiors. But both exist—the one as superior and the other as subject—for the sake of Christ and for the advent in the concrete of his kingdom. As a result, both must seek and find their personal fulfillment by dedicating themselves as functioning members of an organized apostolic community to the work of Christ and of his Church.

Needless to say, these few remarks do not solve all the problems of self-fulfillment in religion; but they do at least place the ideal of self-fulfillment—which is, by the way, a valid and necessary ideal for religious—in a functional context in which it ceases to be an end in itself but is incorporated into the dynamic movement of a whole community toward its corporate fulfillment in Christ.

Functional asceticism could also have a considerable impact upon the relations of religious subjects among themselves. Nominalism tends to foster a kind of Christian Pharisaism, as we have seen. The religious whose nominalistic bent leads him to equate personal holiness apriori with externally rigid observance of the rule cannot but notice, and in some sense to pass judgment upon, the predictable deviations of his brethren. The inevitable violations of charity which result are the commonplaces of common living. Functional asceticism, by modifying the concept of the rule to the extent of conceiving it as a means of perfection to be applied individually, rather than an end to be imposed absolutely, could do much to eliminate the disrupting presence of such pharisaism from religious communities.

In addition, functional asceticism, with its emphasis upon the common enterprise to which superiors and subjects bend their efforts as a working apostolic team, could do much to foster a conscious *esprit de corps* among religious, a sense of belonging and of mutual respect, qualities which are almost completely lacking from the static nominalistic world of routine observance. In such an atmosphere, mutual charity, instead of being centered upon the constant and long-suffering repression of personal annoyance at the faults and irregularities of others, would become the joyful collaboration of dedicated men and women in a common apostolic effort in which petty faults and failings lose importance by comparison with the immensity of the enterprise.

This sense of fellowship and apostolic purpose could in turn give a positive meaning and direction to common exercises of piety, which in a functional approach must be strictly proportioned in both their duration and their content to the concrete aims and needs of the particular religious community in which they are practiced. For important as it truly is, the mere practice of common prayer will never by itself form a united religious community. A united community is not, as a strict nominalism might suggest, simply a community in which every individual does exactly the same things in the same places at the same times. Rather, it is a community dynamically united by its joint action for a common purpose. Common exercises of piety will take on genuine religious meaning only when they become the expression of the conscious purpose shared by each member of the community.

Moreover, by conceiving common spiritual exercises as a means to effective apostolic piety rather than as an end to be imposed absolutely, functional asceticism would also make room for a considerable degree of option as to both the form and the amount of common prayer necessary and useful for each individual religious to foster in himself, in accordance with his personal spiritual needs, an ever deeper awareness of the meaning and purpose of the apostolic enterprise of which he is a part. Common prayer would thus become involved in a constant but relatively fluid dialectic of purposeful activity and purposeful repose: the common activity on the one hand giving rise to the need for common prayer and animating it by its common purpose; common prayer, on the other hand, ever deepening and sustaining the religious community's consciousness of the single purpose which is the bond of unity within all its diverse activities. For while it is true that without any common prayer at all a religious community can easily lose its sense of oneness, still, without the daily lived experience of a common purpose to give rise to the need for common prayer and provide its specific content and direction, community devotions will all too quickly degenerate into the merest formal show. There are in existence house liturgists who have here, I think, matter well worth their reflection.

What is true of prayer in common is true analogously of private prayer as well. The method and duration of private meditation and other personal devotions must be proportioned to the real personal needs of each religious and the spiritual demands of the specific work in which he is engaged. The wise requirements of religious rules for regular periods of quiet and reflection should, therefore, be applied realistically according to individual needs and not imposed universally and blindly.

Functional asceticism could also do much to change our basic image of the spiritual director. Nominalism tends to cast the spiritual director in the role of a professional busybody. Endowed with a special "grace of office," he becomes in a nominalistic framework that person who is divinely commissioned to give official sanction and interpretation to the interior movements of one's soul. Complete openness to him is necessary, therefore, in order that the sure norm of authority may find its way into every aspect of one's personal life.

The results of such a conception of the role of the spiritual director can sometimes be quite disastrous for his spiritual charges. It can, for instance, engender in them a kind of spiritual infantilism in which they constantly seek to shift the responsibility for their every decision onto their advisor. As a result, they soon become all but incapable of making even the most basic personal evaluations on their own. It can also become an unending source of scruples and unnecessary guilt feelings for those religious who, falling short of the unattainable nominalistic ideal of total openness (how can any religious ever hope to communicate to another all that goes on inside him?), remain haunted by the thought of their own spiritual pride or by the fear that they may have strayed from the sure path of approved holiness.

90

A Functional Approach to Ascetical Renewal

Even apart from the dangers of infantilism and scrupulosity, the nominalistic ideal of the spiritual director presupposes as a basic condition of its success that the director is himself an ideal—or at least a competent—one and that there are no real problems of even basic communication between directors and their charges. In point of fact, not all directors are ideal, however; and many problems of communication do exist, as religious have discovered who have attempted to follow the "sure path" of official but misguided advice for a poorly comprehended problem.

A functional reinterpretation of the role of the spiritual father, on the other hand, would begin by challenging the basic presupposition of the nominalistic versions of his job. That is to say, functional asceticism would question whether the role of the spiritual director is primarily to give the sure sanction of authority to all the secret movements of the heart. Instead, direction would be conceived merely as a useful and often vitally necessary means by which a young religious could achieve an ever growing knowledge of himself and, through self-knowledge and the experience of another, a considerable measure of personal decision and self-direction in the spiritual life. Counselees would be taught to regard openness with the director, not as an end to be sought for its own sake, but as an effective means of ultimately reaching spiritual and personal maturity. At the same time, the sage counsellor, instead of binding his spiritual children to his apron strings, would attempt to teach them more and more effectively to stand on their own two feet in spiritual matters.

Functional asceticism would also correct some of the limitations of a nominalistic approach to the virtues. In a thoroughgoing nominalism, the spiritual life tends to be reduced to a predefined set of approved practices. As a result, the overarching values of spiritual living are eventually converted into codified lists of approved ascetical maxims. Thus, a humble person is one who *always* keeps his eyes lowered, who *never* contradicts superiors, who *always* yields to others, etc. A prudent person is one who *never* violates a rule, who *never* takes risks, who *always* asks permission, etc. A charitable person is one who *always* fosters regular observance, who is *always* present at recreation, etc. A recollected religious is one who *always* observes the rules of silence, who *never* visits the room of another, etc.

But functional asceticism would make a clear distinction between the general goals which are the ultimate purpose of particular ascetical practices and the multitude of ways in which those same goals can find expression and concrete human embodiment according to the specific needs of time and circumstance. It would recognize that the concrete practice of virtue cannot be artificially prescribed for one and all out of the rules of ascetical manuals (even though these rules may have many valid applications). Instead, it would insist that the truly virtuous religious must be vitally responsive to the real values which are at stake in every concrete situation, that a life of genuine virtue must be the creative quest for fidelity to certain apostolic goals, according to the demands of the time and place in which those goals must be achieved.

Functional asceticism could do much to change the tone of the ascetical training given to young religious. Instead of forming them in an artificial prayer life of withdrawal from the secular world and its contaminations, it would teach them one animated by their purpose of transforming the world. It would teach them the need to adapt both the amount and content of their prayer life to the demands of their apostolic work and the rhythm of their concrete day-to-day activities. Instead of a mortification of masochistic self-punishment, they would learn to lead a life of careful self-discipline measured by the needs of charity and of their common apostolate. Instead of a blind and passive acceptance of meaningless disciplinary rules and regulations, they would learn an intelligent initiative in adapting their actions both to the goals of religious living and to the needs of the situation.

It would teach them the apostolic purpose of religious poverty, the meaning and intent of the love which inspires the vow of chastity. And it would teach them both the limits and the necessity of obedience. They would learn that blind obedience is not the ideal form of obedience but only a specific instance of obedience sometimes demanded by a superior's inability to reveal the full reason for a command and justified by the subject's confidence in their common dedication to the same apostolic purpose. Ideally, obedience is not blind but intelligent, a union of mind and heart between superior and subject arising from their common dedication to the same end and their mutual agreement upon the best means humanly available to achieve that end. Functional asceticism would teach the young religious that obedience is not abject and passive submission to another but essentially a dialogue.

Functional asceticism could also introduce a certain suppleness into the use of the sacrament of penance. It would measure the use of the sacrament by its primary purpose, namely, reconciliation with the Church after serious sin. As a consequence it would allow more variation in the frequency of confessions of devotion according to the personal spiritual needs of individual religious. At the same time, it would recognize the utility of confessions of devotion in instilling in religious a sense of the communal dimension of even minor transgressions.

Finally, a functional approach to the religious life could provide American religious with a concrete norm and a specific method for going about the work of renewing their institutes, customs, and rules to fit the needs of a post-conciliar age. Both the method and the norm are absent from the world of ascetical nominalism. In it, all change must be initiated at the top of the bureaucratic ladder. A functional approach to renewal would insist upon the need to re-evaluate customs and institutions against the norm of the concrete apostolic need of the actual situation and would provide creative experimentation as the only ultimately effective method of arriving at new solutions within the framework of intelligent obedience. Even today one can still encounter religious who belligerently regard the effectiveness of Catholic colleges and universities as being beyond all question *for no other reason* than that those institutions carry with them the sanction of higher authority.

Similarly, reform in both clerical and religious dress could also benefit from the insights of a functional asceticism. The nominalistic mind tends to endow the wearing of the habit, cassock, or collar with an exaggerated ritualistic meaning and to surround it with elaborate and artificial taboos. I have even known of one cleric who attempted to prove the immutability of ecclesiastical legislation concerning clerical dress from the "fact" that the cassock is the historical descendant of the seamless robe of Christ!

But there is more to the nominalist's attachment to "traditional" religious garb than the fact of legal sanction. The very oddity of clerical and religious dress is transformed in the nominalistic imagination into a cross to be borne ritualistically by religious: a symbol and a proof of their separation from the "profane" pursuits of the ordinary layman.

By the same token, a functional habit in tune with the times has a symbolic message of its own. "See," its wearer

95

says, "I am very much part of this world, though I am striving to transform it in Christ. For there is nothing which exists which is secular or profane except the sinfulness of men."

Viewed functionally, however, a habit is primarily an official uniform and should be used as uniforms are used. Ordinarily, we Americans are an informal lot and do not go parading about in costumes without some reason for it. In our society there is, then, no need for a dawn-to-dusk wearing of the habit. The official uniform of the order should be worn when the situation calls for a uniform, namely, when the individual is acting officially and publicly in the name of the religious organization of which he or she is a member. Indeed, when the matter is viewed calmly and dispassionately, there is no more reason in an American milieu for religious to be habited at every moment of their waking (or even of their public) existence than there is for army officers and nurses to wear their uniforms off duty.

There are, of course, other specific applications of a functional approach to religious life than the ones suggested in this chapter, but it is to be hoped that the proposals included here are sufficient to show that functional asceticism could do much to bridge the gulf that seems to be widening between the older and the younger generations of religious in this country. At the very least it would provide them both with an initial talking point.

For, whatever his faults, the religious of the new breed

is really asking little enough from those charged with his training. He is asking his seniors to have the honesty and courage to acknowledge the inadequacy of present ecclesiastical structures, the boldness to experiment in the hope of finding better ones; he is asking for recognition of the fact that in our restless society the only certain blunder is to do nothing; he is asking for the humility to risk failure, for the perseverance to keep trying. He is asking, in a word, for the security to be insecure, for a strong enough faith to ask questions, for the trust in God and in his grace necessary to the exploration of a new frontier of religious experience.

Unfortunately, for a man formed in a nominalistic tradition, even these basic demands of the new breed are apt to appear overwhelming. For the out-and-out nominalist is woefully lacking in that one quality which all of these demands presuppose: intellectual security. At the heart and soul of nominalism is a radical mistrust of human reason. This was so at its inception, and it has not changed today. As a result, the modern religious will all too often find himself in need of the special kind of spiritual stamina that these revolutionary times demand of us. It is to one of the basic problems of the period of transition through which we are passing that we will attempt to address ourselves in the following chapter.

4 / SELF-FULFILLMENT IN RELIGION

IF THERE is any single problem which seems to be preoccupying young American religious at the present time it is the problem of self-fulfillment. We have almost reached the point where it is impossible to visit a house of formation without either discussing the issue or being subjected to a lecture on it by an intensely serious young religious. In a sense, this situation is understandable enough. Self-fulfillment is, after all, a basic human problem; and American religious, being very human indeed, are understandably concerned about it.

What is new in the contemporary situation, however, is a certain frantic, at times almost hysterical, preoccupation with the question. Yet not even this need be a cause for serious alarm. For here again, I believe, American religious are only reflecting in their own way the frenetic quest of their lay contemporaries for a sense of personal wholeness to enable them to transcend the fragmentation which pervades our lives and the complex society in which we live. It is not surprising, then, that religious today should want to identify holiness with wholeness and an integrated life with the goal of Christian living.

101

Functional Asceticism

Still, in addition to the problems which beset all twentieth-century living, there are certain developments in recent Catholic theological thinking which have, I believe, somewhat complicated the issue insofar as it touches the lives of religious. Ecclesiology has in recent years made immense forward strides. One particularly fruitful line of reflection, stemming ultimately from Pauline teaching on the Mystical Body, has been the effort to distinguish specific missions and functions within the Church corresponding to the different levels of the Church's visible social structure. Much, for example, has been written on the specific contributions of the hierarchy, of religious, and of laymen to the mission of the Church as a whole.

One idea which has emerged from this discussion and is, I think, relevant to the present problem of religious self-fulfillment is that the mission of the Catholic layman should be characterized as an "incarnational" one, as opposed to the mission of the religious, which is—at least, according to some—best described as "eschatological."

The thinking behind this view seems to be that laymen and religious are distinguished from each other primarily by the fact that the former live in the secular world and are immersed in its activities, while the latter have as their vocation the renunciation of the world through the three vows of religion and withdrawal from the things which preoccupy laymen into the quiet and contemplation of the cloister. As a consequence the mission of the layman becomes the gradual transformation of the modern

102

Self-Fulfillment in Religion

secular world through a life lived in Christian faith and love, while the mission of religious with its predefined withdrawal from the world becomes the renunciation of the good things of this life as an act of public witness to the Church's hope in the eschatological fulfillment of the promises of Christ. For Our Lord has assured us that anyone giving up family and possessions for his sake will not go without a reward.

At first encounter, this distinction seems to be a valid one. Religious do not ordinarily hold jobs like laymen. They do not raise families. They do not have personal possessions. Why not speak, then, of their life as being one of eschatological hope rather than of incarnational creativity?

But here a difficulty arises. For if the religious life is essentially other-worldly, is it truly meaningful to speak of self-fulfillment in religion? Eschatological fulfillment would seem by definition to come in eternity, not in time. Must we not conclude, then, that the only self-fulfillment possible for religious is that which they will experience at the moment of death and at the second coming of Christ? This conclusion is, however, far from being self-evident; and it is precisely at this point that the young American religious spontaneously pauses in perplexity. Is it really true to say that there is nothing more to the religious life than the deliberate preference of suffering and misery in this world in the hope of getting a higher place in the next? And if not, if there is a more positive aspect to religious life, then how does it fit in with the proposed eschatological ideal which contemporary theology reserves for religious? What do the terms "incarnational" and "eschatological" really mean? Are self-fulfillment and eschatological witness ultimately compatible? Isn't it just possible that the religious who looks for self-fulfillment is being somehow selfishly untrue to his or her vocation?

These questions are being asked by religious today, and the problems they pose, though seemingly speculative, are full of practical implications. Perhaps one of the best formulations of the issue that I have encountered was that of a young missionary nun who asked me, "What use have I for an asceticism of self-fulfillment? The life that I look forward to on the missions is not one of self-fulfillment but of self-annihilation. Why talk to me about self-fulfillment? What I need is an asceticism of the cross."

Does a functional approach to the religious life have any light to throw on this perplexing and admittedly complex problem? I think that it does, but first a certain number of dogmatic qualifications are in order.

The attempt to characterize the mission of two distinct groups within the Christian community as being the one "incarnational" and the other "eschatological" involves certain speculative hazards. For one thing, it tends to suggest, because of the very distinctness of the two groups and hence presumably of their two apostolic goals, that "incarnation" and "eschaton" refer to two utterly distinct realities, whereas in fact the two words refer to two distinct aspects of one and the same reality. The Scriptures seem to be quite clear on the point that we are living here and now in the eschaton, in the last age of man, and that this eschaton is itself the product and the prolongation of the incarnation.

There are, moreover, other complicating factors here. Often, I believe, one encounters a certain confused tendency in the popular religious imagination to identify the incarnation of the Word exclusively with the "joyful" mysteries of his conception and birth. Christ did, of course, take on a human nature at his conception, but he did not in the moment of his conception or even at his birth take on the fullness of his humanity. Indeed, Christ may in a true sense be said to have been becoming man during the whole of his lifetime—not that the Word was during his earthly career constantly acquiring a new human nature, but that, having taken to himself a nature which was human and hence dynamically integrated into a temporal cosmos, the Word also took to himself the process by which that human nature reached its ultimate and definitive created fulfillment. St. Luke is quite clear on the fact that Christ in his humanity did *grow* in wisdom and age and grace.

Now, as in the case of every man, the supreme moment of fulfillment for Christ's human nature came precisely at the moment of his death upon the cross, which sealed an irrevocable covenant of love between God and man, between the Father and his incarnate Son. In a very real sense, therefore, the cross and Calvary are themselves essentially incarnational. Moreover, it is the death and glorification of Christ which definitively inaugurate the eschaton, the last age of salvation. For it is from the irrevocable commitment of the incarnate Son to his Father in fidelity and love upon the cross and from the irrevocable and loving response of the Father in the glorious exaltation of his Son that the Spirit of love who proceeds from them both from all eternity has entered in time into the hearts of Christ's faithful, transforming them into that eschatological reality which is his Church and making them sharers in her historical mission to mediate between the definitive inauguration of the eschaton and its definitive consummation on the last day.

But, if the eschaton is essentially incarnational and the incarnation is essentially eschatological, it follows that whatever in the Church is truly incarnational must also be simultaneously eschatological, and vice versa. Hence, neither the mission of the layman nor that of the religious can be characterized as being exclusively either the one or the other.

Indeed, one cannot but suspect that lurking behind the tendency to oppose the incarnational layman to the eschatological religious is the old nominalistic distinction between the "secular" layman immersed in the "profane" things of this world and the "professional" religious dedicated to the "pursuit of perfection" through the performance of a predefined list of "holy" and "religious" acts. The old distinction has, to be sure, been dressed up a bit to fit the modern temper. Instead of being purely profane, the secular world of the layman is in the new terminology open to the transformation of his incarnational activity. But the poor religious is in much the same state as before. Despite the new designation "eschatological," he remains radically segregated from the world of men, immured behind cloistered walls in a life of irrelevant, ritualistic renunciation.

Perhaps the genuinely eschatological nature of the layman's mission may become clearer if we recall that a person is officially constituted a layman of the Church by the performance of two actions of profound eschatological significance, namely, baptism and confirmation. For by baptism a person is officially incorporated into an eschatological community of faith, hope, and love through a sacramental death with Christ to the old Adam and a resurrection with him to newness of life. Confirmation ratifies and strengthens this initial commitment by officially entrusting to the baptized layman the mission of bearing prophetic witness to his faith in the sight of men, despite the sufferings and persecutions which, as Christ has warned, will certainly await all who profess to be his disciples. Hence, in the very acts which confer upon the layman his own special mission in the Church there is present that same explicit element of eschatological renunciation and hope which is essential to every total commitment of Christian faith and love.

Conversely, it is not only the layman but the religious

also who is dedicated by the very nature of his ecclesial mission to the incarnational task of transforming all things in Christ. Indeed, it is the apostolic transformation of human society which is, as I have tried to suggest in the first chapter, the fundamental driving force behind the triple vow of religious renunciation.

We may conclude, then, that in the respective missions of laymen and religious the threads of incarnation and eschaton, of renunciation and fulfillment, of cross and creativity are as inextricably intertwined as they were in the mission of the incarnate Word himself, who came into our midst in order to vindicate God's infinite love for men, but who was forced to bring his offer of divine love into a world marred by man's own sinfulness. For he came to us seeking our at-one-ment, our reconciliation with himself and his Father; but he came with a perfect divine foreknowledge of the consequences of his coming, with a divine prescience of the cross and of Calvary.

Hence, even though the renunciation present in the life of Christ was not the goal of his coming (that goal was the definitive union of mankind with God), still, in a world thrown out of joint by the sinfulness of men, renunciation became a necessary means, a tragically unavoidable step in the final accomplishment of the definitive reconciliation of men with their Maker in a covenant of everlasting love. For the renunciation in the life of Christ is nothing else than the incarnation of a divine love freely offered to an ungrateful humanity. It is Jesus' obedient and gratuitous gift of himself to men in spite of their weakness, in spite of their sinfulness, in spite even of the cross.

It is, then, in the very renunciation of Christ that every Christian—whether cleric, religious, or layman—must find the key unlocking the meaning of the renunciation which must inevitably form an integral part of the Christian commitment. For Christian renunciation is nothing else than our poor struggle to imitate the kenosis of Christ. It is the risk of loving, freely taken and gratuitously bestowed in the name of Christ upon those who are capable of turning such an offer of love into a Calvary. Like the love of Christ, it seeks communion, not the cross. But like the love of Christ, it does not shrink from becoming a crucifixion through the indifference and the malice of men. For it is unshaken in the belief that such love, even so, is truly redemptive, that it is strong with the strength of the risen Lord, and that even in rejection it has already triumphed over the selfishness and malice of men. It was such love as this that St. Ignatius Loyola in his *Spiritual Exercises* called the third degree of humility; for it is the simple willingness to be Christ's fool and to prove our love for him who first loved us even in our sinfulness, by daring to risk loving those who are most in need of love, because in their selfishness and weakness they are the least capable of responding with love in return.

Such love as this is the mission and the sacred trust

of every Christian, and for that reason it cannot be the prerogative of religious alone. It is certainly present in the vows of religion. But it is no less present in the baptismal commitment of every layman. It is present in his prophetic mission to bear witness to Christ in a sinful and faithless world. And it is present also in the very irrevocability of the Christian marriage bond.

But if all of this is true, then can one truly claim that the apostolic mission of a layman in the Church is different from that of a religious? On the face of it, it would seem that we have destroyed any possible basis for any sort of genuine distinction between them. For we claim that the mission of the religious is both incarnational and eschatological; and then we add that the layman's is also. Religious, we say, profess a life of Christian renunciation; but so does the layman. Laymen are called upon to transform the world in Christ; so are religious. The religious is called to a life of perfect love, of meditation, and of prayer; but so, by reason of this baptismal commitment and prophetic mission, is the layman. Religious take vows of poverty, but so in fact can a layman. Where, then, is the difference between the two? Or is there a difference?

There is; but it may not be so great a difference as the external, non-essential, and ritualistic trappings and taboos of religious orders have given us to suppose. Vatican II has been at pains to remind us that the vocation of the layman finds its fulfillment in the vocation to the religious life. It is not surprising, then, that we should find several points of contact between them. Still, the mission of the layman is different, for the witness which the layman bears to his faith in Christ is specifically an *individual* one. His official acceptance as a layman of the Church in baptism is the acceptance of an individual, and the prophetic mission entrusted to him in confirmation comes to him also as an individual. The religious, on the other hand, bears witness to Christ, not merely as an individual, but specifically and by the definitive and all-important commitment of the vow of obedience as a member of an officially approved community of Christians who, under the direction of the hierarchy, have dedicated their persons and all that they possess to the accomplishment of some work of vital importance either to the building up of the Christian community itself or to the extension of that community to persons and lands still outside the fold of Christ. In thus devoting himself professionally to the needs of the Church in an organized community of apostolic service, the religious gives to his life a new and specifically ecclesial dimension which is not in any way opposed to the commitment of the layman but which extends and completes it and lends to it a different incarnational modality.

It seems to me, then, to be a bit misleading to attempt to distinguish the mission of the layman from that of the religious simply on the basis of the fact that laymen hold steady jobs "in the world" and are immersed in the affairs of men. True, the steady job of the religious is with the Church, but when the Church is functioning properly it is immersed in the contemporary human scene. Secular institutes are, for instance, proof enough that religious can also hold jobs "in the world" where the needs of the Church demand it; and even ordinary religious find themselves often enough working side by side with laymen in one and the same undertaking. (Think, for example, of the scientific research of a Teilhard.)

The real difference between the two would seem rather to lie in the fact that whereas the layman bears witness in his job to the faith that is his, he does so precisely as an individual within the Church, while the religious bears witness to the same faith specifically as a member of an approved and functioning apostolic community explicitly dedicated to filling the immediate needs of the whole Christian community as such.

The individual character of the layman's witness remains essentially intact even when his personal interest in Church affairs leads him to join some official lay organization, for membership in such an organization remains accidental and peripheral to the basic structure of his life as a Christian. It is precisely as an individual that he freely donates his time to the work of the organization, all the while maintaining the right to break off relations with it whenever, as an individual, he may see fit to do so. Nevertheless, the existence of such service organizations for laymen in the Church is only another indication of the basic continuity underlying the lay and the religious vocation.

But even granting the validity of our argument up to this point, what has all this got to do with the original problem of self-fulfillment in religion? Quite a bit, really. For one thing, our reflections help to make it clear that self-fulfillment is as legitimate an object of concern for religious men and women as it is for any layman and that there is no more reason to postpone the personal fulfillment of religious exclusively until the life to come than there is in the case of any other Christian. In other words, the remark quoted above of the young missionary nun who said she needed an asceticism of the cross rather than one of self-fulfillment was actually only half true. In point of fact she, along with every other Christian, actually needs both. A missionary who can find no personal sense of fulfillment in the work of bringing the gospel of Christ to foreign lands will, I seriously suspect, ultimately prove to be a dubious asset at best to the mission to which he is assigned.

At the same time, we must also conclude that every Christian quest for self-fulfillment must be a realistic one. For the cross of Christ stands before each of us as a portent and as a prophecy that in a world alienated from God by sin, perfect self-fulfillment in this life is impossible for any man. Anyone who professes to follow in the footsteps of a crucified Savior must face the simple fact that in a world like ours the only possible path to self-fulfillment remains the free and gratuitous offer of oneself to others in love even when the only foreseeable response to that offer is repudiation and rejection.

It is also a bit clearer, as a result of our reflections, how a religious is to go about the business of seeking genuine

113

self-fulfillment. For a religious, as we have seen, is a person with a purpose, one who has dedicated his life and his talents to the needs of the Church and to the accomplishment of its work. In other words, it is total self-dedication to the service of the Church which constitutes for a religious the concrete embodiment of his personal self-offering in love to God, to his Christian brethren, and to all mankind. It is, therefore, in their response to his love that he must experience whatever self-fulfillment is possible to him in this life.

The problem of self-fulfillment in religion is, then, clearly a multidimensional one. It involves not only the individual religious himself with his personal history, talents, limitations, and aspirations but also his relationships with the members of his own religious community and with those among whom he works.

Moreover, a religious vocation is not at all an abstract thing. Indeed, ascetical writers have always insisted correctly that it is a personal call from God. Seen from the viewpoint of the religious himself, it involves the personal commitment of an *individual* to a *particular* order or congregation and hence in most cases to a *particular kind* of apostolic work for which he judges himself to be suited. Conversely, from the viewpoint of the order or congregation, a religious vocation implies the acceptance of a *particular individual* with his personal talents, background, limitations, and aspirations as being actually fitted for the particular kind of work to which the order itself is dedicated.

114

In other words, the religious vocation implies a mutual commitment of love both on the part of the individual religious and on the part of the other members of his order and the superiors which govern it. On the one hand, the individual religious not only binds himself to a life of service to others as a member of his religious community but also pledges himself to accept as his brethren the other members of that community who are dedicated like himself to the same apostolic enterprise. On the other hand, the order or congregation in its members and superiors not only binds itself in love and friendship to the individual religious as an individual, but pledges itself to see that he shall be able to use his talents to the fullest extent possible in the service of Christ and of his Church.

Self-fulfillment becomes a problem in religion when either the religious himself or the order, or both, fall short of this initial commitment of love.

This can happen in a number of ways. On the part of the religious, failure frequently takes the form of slow surrender to egotism and selfishness which gradually corrodes the purity of the initial self-offering and substitutes the love of self for the free gift of oneself to others in love. Yet frequently enough, I fear, this gradual decline in generosity on the part of individual religious is itself the result of the day-to-day failure of the other members of the order and of its superiors to live up completely to their own commitment. One wonders how many souls who have generously consecrated themselves and all they

115

have to God and to his Church have allowed their lives to become paralyzed by bitterness and self-pity simply because they have never truly been accepted by their own religious brethren or because superiors have in the press of circumstances, or in too much zeal for the rule and the needs of the order's institutions and not enough zeal for the needs of its members, assigned them to work for which they had no aptitude or to posts which gave no scope to their talent.

Does a functional approach to the religious life have any light to shed on this difficult problem? I am inclined to think that it does. For as we have already seen, it is precisely here at the level of interpersonal relationships among religious that a nominalistic asceticism can wreak its greatest spiritual havoc. Indeed, in a thoroughgoing nominalism the problem of personal self-fulfillment scarcely exists. If it is faced at all, its solution is quickly reduced to a single devastating syllogism: self-fulfillment in religion consists in doing the will of God; *atqui* the will of God is the officially sanctioned rule of one's order and the equally sanctioned will of one's superior; *ergo,* self-fulfillment in religion consists in exact and unquestioning submission to the rule and in total and passive compliance with the will of the superior.

The abstract logic is clear enough, and sometimes with the right superior and the right subject it even works in practice. But when it fails in practice, its failure can truly be spectacular. For often enough a religious, whether he is a superior or a subject, is forced to deal with indi-

116

viduals as such, with their personal needs in specific situations; and unfortunately a strict nominalist has nothing in his mental equipment to enable him to cope with the particular as particular.

The problem can become especially grave when a religious with serious personal needs is forced to deal with a superior who is of a predominantly nominalistic cast of mind. For however good his intentions, such a superior is incapable of that full response of love to the individual precisely as an individual which in the circumstances happens to be the one thing necessary. An analogous problem, though perhaps not so serious, may occur when the size of a religious house or province makes any personal relationship between superior and subject a practical impossibility.

But the dangers to self-fulfillment in religion do not lie exclusively on the side of superiors. A nominalistic subject can often be an even greater source of danger and unhappiness to himself and to the people with whom he or she must live. One must deal officially with superiors only occasionally, but one must live with oneself and with one's religious peers on a day-to-day basis. As a result, the spirit of rigid pharisaism engendered by a nominalistic ascetical formation can easily become an endless source of spiritual sterility to the religious imbued with it and of constant anguish and pain to those with whom he or she must deal.

Needless to say, there are no simple solutions to the problem of self-fulfillment in religion. Precisely because it is a personal problem, it requires as many solutions as there are people in religious life. What we do need, however, is a spiritual and ascetical formation for religious which will allow each of them, with the help of God's grace, to find that measure of true self-fulfillment possible to him in a Church and among men who are still in dreadful need of the grace of Christ and of his redemption.

A functional approach to the religious life could, I believe, do much to provide such an atmosphere. For one thing, it would give to religious life a sense of purpose which is largely denied it in a nominalistic frame of reference. One of the key characteristics of nominalism is its tendency to separate institutional structures from the goals which give them life and meaning and thus to convert them from means to ends in themselves. Indeed, a large measure of the current concern of American religious with the problem of self-fulfillment stems, I believe, from a feeling, often perhaps only on the threshold of consciousness, that they are dedicating their lives not so much to the vital needs of the American Church of the sixties as to the bolstering of a tottering and increasingly irrrelevant bureaucratic structure which is incapable of any but the most superficial self-criticism and apostolic adaptation. Such feelings may in fact prove ungrounded in many instances; but where they exist they must be met with a spirit of ruthless self-scrutiny and vigorous experimentation at an institutional level.

Self-Fulfillment in Religion

It is precisely at this point that a functional asceticism with its insistence upon the need for carefully distinguishing means from ends could provide a frame of reference in which the concrete problems of institutional adaptation to the contemporary scene could be discussed frankly and handled intelligently by superiors and subjects alike.

Moreover, by de-absolutizing the rule and by focusing authority explicitly on the maximum apostolic effectiveness of each member of the religious community, functional asceticism would make the full exploitation of the talents of each individual member of the religious community not only the legitimate concern but the duty in conscience of both superiors and subjects alike. Thus it could also provide a frame of reference in which both superiors and subjects could, when the need arose, look beyond the immediate needs of the institutional commitments of their particular order or congregation and allow individuals with exceptional talents full freedom and scope to develop them for Christ and for his Church outside of the fixed and ordinarily necessary framework provided by traditional institutional structures.

Furthermore, by fostering a sense of common purpose which transcends the routine fulfillment of rules and regulations, functional asceticism could do much to encourage among religious a genuine interest in and concern for one another. For the feeling of being part of a meaningful enterprise tends automatically to produce within a group

119

an atmosphere of mutual acceptance, love, and friendship which are essential ingredients of self-fulfillment in any walk of life.

In addition, functional asceticism would also make it clear that the commitment of obedience is not the purely passive acceptance of the rules and institute of one's order. For just as incorporation into the Church brings to each individual Christian the personal responsibility of seeing to it that the Church becomes and remains a vital force in the lives of men, so too the commitment of the vow of obedience brings to each member of a religious order or congregation the personal responsibility of seeing to it that that order or congregation itself becomes and remains an effective apostolic instrument in the work of the Church.

Finally, a functional approach to the religious life would justify the need in every religious order, congregation, province, and house for a permanent and effective structural apparatus for airing, at a local, provincial, or universal level, any possible changes and adaptations which may be demanded by circumstances; some sort of public forum in which problems can be faced by members as a group, opinions expressed publicly, and solutions reached by those in authority which correspond as far as possible not only to the needs of the situation but to the concrete aspirations of the members of the order themselves.

This last suggestion is important enough to need further development.

5 / DEMOCRATIC STRUCTURES AND RELIGIOUS LIFE

IF ASCETICAL RENEWAL among religious is to be thorough-going, it cannot remain limited to the level of personal and individual piety but must find some sort of institu-tionalized expression. At the end of the last chapter we seemed to be suggesting that such institutionalized re-newal might well take the form of a certain "democratiza-tion" of American religious life. To religious whose insti-tute is basically monarchical in structure, such a proposal might seem to be not merely unusual but even quite shocking. However, the members of older religious or-ders whose basic governmental structure is capitular (and hence more democratic) will be quick to realize that nothing more is involved than the extension and expan-sion of democratic structures already existing within the approved framework of institutionalized religious living.

There is no reason why the structural modification of religious institutes should be a source of scandal to their members. Religious orders are themselves nothing else than the institutionalized prolongation of the charismatic inspiration of their founders. It is fitting, then, that any genuinely charismatic movement of grace within an estab-

123

lished order or congregation should likewise find expression in the functional modification and adaptation of its traditional institutions. Such useful and necessary structural changes should be regarded as fundamentally continuous with the charismatic movement of grace originated by the order's founder. For it is one and the same Spirit who dispenses his charismatic gifts at every age of the Church's history; and surely he who was powerful enough to raise up the founder of an order to meet the apostolic needs of the Church at a given point in her historical evolution is wise and powerful enough to enlighten religious at every era in their order's development to find the means necessary to adapt the organization of their order to meet the vital needs of a changing apostolic situation. Surely, also, the original intention of any genuinely charismatic leader must have been that the institution which he had founded should always remain a vital and effective force within the Christian community and that its formal structure should correspond to the actual needs of God's people.

Religious should, therefore, be extremely wary of interpreting official admonitions concerning the need for fidelity to one's institute in any sort of narrow nominalistic sense. To the nominalistic mind, fidelity to one's institute means blind preservation of institutions and practices which bear the past sanction of authority and tradition, irrespective of their relevance to the present apostolic situation. By contrast, in a functional approach to re-

124

ligious life, fidelity to one's institute is nothing else than fidelity to the basic Christian values and goals which that institute is attempting to embody—but according to the concrete demands of time and circumstance. Hence, in a functional context, true fidelity to one's institute necessarily includes a frank recognition that the specific means which religious founders may have hit upon to reach the constitutive goals of their order are historically conditioned not only by the circumstances in which the order was founded but also by the personal, psychological, and theological limitations of the founder himself, whatever his degree of personal sanctity.

We cannot, therefore, exclude the possibility of expanding the democratic structure of American religious orders apriori, simply on the basis of the fact that up till now their institutes have made only limited provision for such structures. The history of this country is short, according to the standards of salvation history; and most religious rules and institutes are in one way or another based on rather ancient European models. It is not impossible, therefore, that we have actually reached a point in the development of the American Church when the results of our national political experience can be turned to advantage in at least partially restructuring American orders in an adapted democratic mould.

But however hopeful such a suggestion may appear at first sight, its ultimate acceptability and consequences are far from being self-evident. Indeed, one can mount some rather telling arguments against the legitimacy and the prudence of any such "democratizing" efforts within the American Church.

To begin with, religious orders are a visible extension of the hierarchical structure of the universal Church, and the Church is not and can never be a democracy in the strict sense of the term. For democracy is a type of self-government which is based on the principle that it is the people themselves whom God has ultimately invested with civil authority. Democracy presupposes, then, that elected officials receive from the people both the power to govern and the obligation to do so according to the people's own will. But the Church is by contrast a super-natural society which has resulted from the gratuitous intervention of God in the course of human history. The authority to govern invested in her rulers derives, there-fore, not from the faithful themselves, but from Christ, the incarnate Son of God, who freely and lovingly se-lected twelve men from his disciples to be the pillars of a new Israel and gave them the power to teach, govern, and sanctify in his name.

Today, of course, the pope and bishops, the successors of the apostles, exercise that same power over the Church in the name of Christ; and religious must be subject in their apostolic work either to the local bishop or, in the case of the religious orders, to the bishop of Rome him-self, the head of the episcopal college and its source of unity. Clearly, then, the authority present in religious

126

orders is not democratic in the ordinary political sense of the term, and one should never aspire to make it so. Moreover, any system of checks and balances similar to that in our national government would seem at first sight to have no place in an organization whose authority is of direct divine institution.

But there are still further difficulties confronting any effort to "democratize" the Church. Matters of faith and morals can never be decided simply on the basis of a popular vote. Our own history shows that those American Protestant denominations who have attempted to reach dogmatic decisions through popular democratic processes have ended in fragmentation and doctrinal contradictions.

Christianity is based on the unshakable principle that it is God, not man, who makes religion, and that in the person of his incarnate Son, God has spoken his definitive historical word of salvation to the world. Now, no reflective person would ever conceive of trying to solve a problem in American history by holding a popular referendum in all fifty states. The interpretation of the events of our common historical heritage must be left in the hands of those who are trained and competent in this sphere. Hence, analogously, the religious meaning of the events of salvation history through which God speaks his saving word of grace to man cannot be left to the whims of any electorate but must be decided by those who are competent. But the only people who are completely competent to interpret the meaning of God's self-revelation

127

to men in a definitive fashion are those who have received the mission and the authority from Christ himself to do so in his name—that is, the pope speaking officially as the head of the episcopal college or the college of bishops teaching officially in union with the pope who is their head. The very nature of revelation itself would seem, then, to preclude the possibility of democratic structures within the Church.

Nevertheless, these two "anti-democratic" arguments based on the structure of the Church as established by Christ and on the nature of revelation, while completely valid up to a point, should not be pushed beyond their proper limits. For while it is true that the Church is not a democracy, it is equally true that it is not a despotism either. In conferring authority upon the apostles, Christ made it quite clear to them on more than one occasion that in his Church the exercise of authority is a service to be rendered to God's people, not a privilege to be exacted from them, that those who were his plenipotentiary ambassadors to the world, his apostles, were to become as little children and the least of all, in order to win all, through humility and love, to Christ.

Now, precisely because the exercise of authority in the Church is a service to be rendered to the community and not an end in itself, the authority conferred by Christ upon the rulers of his Church is essentially a functional thing. It exists for a purpose. And the mere fact that it comes from God and carries a divine sanction does not alter its essentially functional nature.

128

Ecclesiastical authority does, then, in spite of its supernatural origin, display certain specific analogies with ordinary civil authority. Like civil authority it exists for the sake of the common good of those over whom it is exercised; in its case, to mediate to them the saving grace of Christ. Moreover, all authority, whether civil or ecclesiastical, comes from God. Hence, what truly distinguishes ecclesiastical authority is not its divine origin but rather its incarnational and sacramental character. Ecclesiastical authority is an effect and a prolongation of the redemptive mission of the Word made flesh, and as a sacramental manifestation of the presence of his grace in the world enjoys, under certain conditions, special privileges, such as infallibility or sacramental efficacy, which are absent from the exercise of merely civil power. But note well that these very privileges are themselves functional in intent, efficacious means taken by God to ensure the accomplishment of that graced service which is the constitutive goal of Church authority.

It is the very functional nature of ecclesiastical authority which makes it possible to introduce into Catholicism certain modified and adapted versions of democratic civil structures in order to assist those invested with divine authority in the accomplishment of their appointed mission. But here we must move very cautiously, as the Protestant experience in this country has taught us well.

To begin with, it is interesting and instructive to note that religious orders have manifested a discernible dialectical movement in their "democratic" development.

129

Functional Asceticism

The thetic moment of this dialectic took form during the Middle Ages. Born and nurtured in a religiously stable and Christianized environment, the major medieval orders found in capitular government not only an apt expression of the communal nature of religious life but also an effective means of government well suited to the relatively slow and stable rhythm of the agricultural society of medieval Europe.

Significantly enough, the structural antithesis to capitular government appeared upon the historical scene during the course of the dissolution of the medieval cultural complex. Ignatius Loyola, the founder of the Jesuit order, on being faced with the sudden expansion of the confines of the known world and the rapid disintegration and fragmentation of what had once been a united Christian Europe, repudiated the capitular principle as apostolically inopportune and opted instead for a basically monarchical form of government for his order. (Even in the Society of Jesus, however, certain remnants of capitular government still remain.) What is of interest to us here is that Ignatius did so for explicitly functional reasons. Given the dire apostolic needs of his times, he judged government by chapter to be a democratic luxury that the religious of his order could ill afford. Instead, he cut through the redtape of the older, slower-moving capitular forms and replaced them with an efficient chain of command moving downward from the pope through the Jesuit general to the provincials and local superiors. In the traditional but sometimes misinterpreted metaphor, his religious were to be the "spiritual light cavalry" of the papacy, capable of being sent on a moment's notice to any part of the world where the greater glory of God demanded their presence. (Still, Ignatius intended the government of his order to be neither monolithic nor militaristic but paternal; and he insists on the need for free and constant communication between superiors and subjects.)

The subsequent history of the Counter-Reformation actually justified the validity of these then revolutionary modifications of what had come to be considered the traditional structure of religious orders. The new mobility and military discipline of the Jesuits made them the scourge of the heretical forces, and the champions of reform within the Church; and it placed them in the vanguard of the Church's immense new missionary effort.

As a result, the rule of the Jesuit order became a model frequently copied by the subsequent founders of new religious congregations and institutes.

The fact that the post-Reformation Church has moved from her medieval position of political and spiritual ascendancy to her present status of enduring diaspora, the constant presence of the Communist threat, the plight of the emerging new nations, the crying needs of the Church in South and Central America, the rapid rhythm of modern society—these and other factors would seem to indicate that the monarchical principle enunciated by

Ignatius is in its basic insight still apostolically and functionally relevant, that the orders still need the mobility and freedom for apostolic work which a monarchical system provides.

Nevertheless, a complete functional assessment of the present apostolic situation would also seem to indicate that the time may well be approaching for a third, synthetic moment in the democratic development of religious orders. The world has changed considerably since Ignatius founded the Jesuits. Vatican II has brought the spiritual atmosphere of the Counter-Reformation to an end. The principle of collegiality, the decree on the Eastern Churches, and the very freedom of discussion of the Council Fathers themselves have all made it clear to Catholics everywhere that within the unity of Roman Catholicism there is room for a great deal of legitimate local diversity. Moreover, religious orders have themselves grown in the course of time to world-wide dimensions, with the inevitable result that any sort of exaggerated centralization or insistence upon rigid, bureaucratic uniformity is bound to hinder rather than to help their apostolic work.

Needless to say, it is far beyond the scope and the intention of this book to attempt any sort of detailed analysis of the specific structural modifications which the changing apostolic situation may demand of particular orders and congregations. But this much at least seems clear. If the monarchical principle of religious government enunciated by Ignatius Loyola at the time of the

132

Reformation is to remain functionally relevant, it must be supplemented in our day by controlled decentralization and by controlled experimentation and adaptation at a local, regional, and national level.

Moreover, once one has granted in principle the legitimacy of a certain amount of national diversity, not only within the Church as a whole but also within one and the same religious order, it is not difficult to envisage the possibility of developing gradually and experimentally among American religious some useful democratic structures which would assist and not compromise the actual exercise of authority on the part of American religious superiors.

It is important at this point to recall that not every exercise of ecclesiastical authority is a privileged one. Not every act of doctrinal or moral instruction bears the stamp of infallibility. Not every word uttered in the Church is an efficacious sacramental word.

The nature of the privileged exercise of ecclesiastical authority has been forever fixed by Christ and can never be changed or "democratized." But the vast majority of the day-to-day decisions of those in authority in the Church are not, as a matter of fact, privileged. They must be reached carefully and painfully through the exercise of ordinary human prudence. Now, every valid prudential judgment must be both well-informed and morally sound. And it is precisely at this prudential level of day-to-day decision-making that certain modified democratic structures could be immensely useful to American ec-

133

clesiastical authorities in formulating sound policy and reaching apt and relevant conclusions.

For example, the complexification of twentieth-century society makes it inevitable that within the Church there should exist distinct groups with legitimate vested interests. Since the purpose of ecclesiastical authority is to serve God's people in the name of Christ, and not to lord it over them, it should be obvious that here in America at least a situation is developing in which there is a growing need to establish some sort of permanent apparatus of communication *within the Catholic community* which would enable different groups within the Church to present their needs and problems effectively to legitimate ecclesiastical authority. That the representatives of such a group should be elected by its members is also, in this country at least, both suitable and, by the common-sense experience of life in a democratic society, ultimately the most efficient way of proceeding.

To be a bit more specific, it has become of vital importance to the daily conduct of Church affairs that Church leaders should maintain constant contact with different racial, cultural, and economic groups within the Catholic community and that this contact should not be haphazard or left to the personal whim of those in authority but should be so institutionalized as to make regular interchanges an effective and unavoidable means of continuing dialogue.

What is true of the Church as a whole in this country is likewise true of religious orders as well, particularly of

134

orders and houses in which the large number of religious subjects makes contact with superiors irregular, impersonal, and inefficient. In such relatively large and complex communities, it is often easy for a superior, through sheer ignorance of the thoughts and aspirations of the many different groups within the house, to become aligned in his own thinking and decisions with one particular group whose vested interests may not coincide with the needs of the community as a whole, or with other groups within the same religious house. When that happens, the institutional mechanism of officially appointed consultors or of personal manifestations of conscience is frequently an inadequate channel of truly effective dialogue. I know, for instance, of one superior of a community of nearly two hundred subjects who complained that whenever a decision of importance which concerned the whole community came up, about five people would come in and tell him one thing, five others would come in and tell him something completely different, and out of the nearly two hundred religious in the house only ten would come in to tell him anything at all. In such a situation (and the community need not be as large as this for the situation to exist) permanent elected spokesmen charged with the task of discovering the thoughts and needs of different groups within the community, through organized surveys of opinion if necessary, can do much to keep superiors well-informed concerning the changing concrete needs and aspirations of their subjects.

There is, moreover, no reason why such a communications board of democratically elected representatives need be restricted to the level of religious houses alone. Provincials and other higher superiors could learn much about their provinces and subjects were such permanent boards set up, even if it were for no other purpose than the regular conduct of surveys of opinion among the members of an order or province concerning the problems which are of common interest, either to all or at least to the members of some particular group within the religious family. Besides keeping superiors informed, such surveys could also help to bring religious subjects themselves to some sort of concrete awareness of the terrible complexities involved in the government of a religious province or house.

Another effective means of mobilizing the resources of a religious community is regular group discussions and brainstorming sessions for coping imaginatively with problems of common interest. Needless to say, complete freedom of speech without restriction or reprisal, but with a strong emphasis on the positive and the constructive, is essential to any such effort in group dynamics.

But merely keeping the channels of communication open is not enough. Mere representation to superiors is inadequate unless subjects have some sort of genuine confidence that superiors are themselves under the acknowledged obligation to take whatever action is appropriate to the represented need. How very much of the smooth running of religious orders depends upon the

136

ability of a superior to instill confidence in his subjects that every available means is being employed to meet the present need!

Permanent boards of elected spokesmen representing the different groups within a religious family could perform in this respect an important prophetic function within their order or congregation by reminding superiors in all meekness and charity of those needs which have indeed been represented, but have as yet gone unfulfilled. They could also aid superiors in channeling back to subjects, when it is found to be necessary or useful, information concerning the obstacles which superiors may be encountering from an administrative point of view in trying to implement their subjects' suggestions. Such regular give-and-take between superiors and subjects at an institutional level can, when it is carried on in a spirit of mutual respect and love, serve not only as a useful, but often as a necessary, supplement to individual personal contact between them.

Finally, there is no apparent reason why the representatives to general or provincial congregations could not be chosen through some sort of process of popular election by the members of an order rather than by an outmoded seniority system in those orders in which such systems do still survive. It must be taken into account here that penicillin and other wonder drugs seem to be having a side-effect of converting more than one religious family into a species of gerontocracy. There are, of course, a great many religious around who are both old and wise and up-to-date, and whose wisdom and experience can be of much benefit to their orders. But the fact remains that in past ages when men had a more limited life span, there was a much better chance that the older members of an order would be vigorous and in touch with the affairs and needs of the province than is the case today with our longer lease on life combined with our accelerated rate of cultural change and development. As a result, a seniority system for determining the representatives of important deliberative bodies is all too apt to be both inefficient and obsolete.

Needless to say, the proposals made in this chapter are only proposals. The functional key to all such attempts at adapting democratic structures to the needs of the Church and of religious orders must be prudent experimentation followed by periods of critical reflection. For only by the constant interplay of reflection and practice is continued progress at an institutional level ever really possible.

6 / PROSPECT AND RETROSPECT

THE BEST PART OF CLIMBING a hill comes at the moment when the climber, after reaching the top, turns around to survey the path of his ascent. There is really nothing new for him to see: every object which lined the way to the top he had inspected during the climb from close at hand. But there is a great deal that is new *about* what he sees. For viewing the sights of his climb in retrospect and within the framework of a much larger perspective, he suddenly sees them in a way in which he could not have seen them before; and hence he may in a true sense be said to see them for the first time.

As we approach the end of our reflections, it might perhaps be useful for us to imitate the climber, to reverse our field of vision and view in retrospect the thoughts which have been preoccupying us in the preceding chapters. In so doing, we shall not attempt to introduce any new ideas into our field of vision, but by reviewing in inverse order some of the high points of our previous reflections on the religious life, we shall perhaps be able to see them from a new vantagepoint and in a somewhat enlarged frame of reference. This may in turn permit us

141

a kind of penetration into them which has eluded us at closer range.

We began our reflections with the consciousness of a crisis which is brewing in American religious orders and congregations—a growing rift, a lack of communication and understanding among religious, particularly between the older and younger generations. We judged the speculative roots of this disturbance to lie in great measure in a misguided effort to force the legitimate spiritual aspirations of American religious into the largely irrelevant and artificial mould of an outmoded ascetical ideal. This diagnosis set us off upon a path of reflection which terminated in an effort to qualify some recent theological suggestions concerning the purpose of religious life in general. The time has come, then, to re-situate our original problem within the framework of these more general reflections.

We have suggested that the effort to characterize the mission of the layman, on the one hand, as positive, creative, and incarnational and the mission of the religious, on the other, as negative, renunciatory, and eschatological leads, when pushed too far, to too narrow a notion of incarnation and eschaton and ultimately to a distortion of the apostolic mission of both laymen and religious. It suggests, for instance, that the incarnation was not also a kenosis of the Word of God, that it contained no element of renunciation in it, and that the eschaton is exclusively negative and other-worldly.

142

We have seen, however, that the renunciation present in the life of Christ is the incarnation of divine love offered persistently and triumphantly to men in spite of their sinful rejection of it. And we have seen that the eschaton, even though it will be accomplished definitively on the last day, has already been definitively inaugurated in time and that it is in time that men must work out under God's grace their ultimate eschatological destiny.

We have concluded, therefore, that the life of every Christian must necessarily be both incarnational and eschatological, a mixture of renunciation and creativity, that it is not religious alone who are to live lives of Christian renunciation, but that in the case of religious the renunciation which is necessarily present in every Christian commitment achieves, through the vow of obedience in particular, an explicit ecclesial dimension. Moreover, in the context of Christian living, this renunciation is never exclusively other-worldly in its intention. If it is truly Christian, it must seek at least the partial fulfillment of love in this life through the incarnational construction of Christ's kingdom here on earth, so that religious renunciation (like all Christian renunciation) parallels at a graced level the renunciation that is the basic presupposition of all human creativity.

Hence, we have also concluded that the religious life when properly understood must be characterized as essentially creative and positive. Its constitutive purpose is creative dedication to fulfilling the needs of God's

143

people; and even though it is conscious that ultimate and perfect human fulfillment must be reserved for the life to come, still it seeks to bring about in this life that fulfillment of Christian communion in love which Christ proclaimed to be the mark of his true disciples.

Moreover, because the witness of the religious is explicitly ecclesial, this creative goal of religious living must be achieved corporately, through the co-operative effort of a Christian community of apostolic endeavor. Hence, we have concluded, *everything in the religious community* must be measured and judged by the concrete needs of the immediate apostolic situation—including the aspirations of its members, its rules, the institutional structures of the order or congregation, even the decisions of legitimate authority, which in the very act of uniting, co-ordinating, and directing the apostolic witness of the community endows it with its specifically ecclesial dimension.

We have seen furthermore that since even the decisions of authority must be measured and judged by the concrete purpose which must ultimately justify the very existence of that authority, it follows necessarily that each religious, in virtue of his vow of obedience which consecrates him to the fulfillment of that purpose, receives the responsibility of bearing mature prophetic witness, when it is necessary within his own order, to the need for change and apostolic adaptation at a personal and at an institutional level.

144

We are thus forced to conclude that nominalistic asceticism gives at best a partial picture of religious life. It is correct in insisting on the importance of authority; but to the extent that ascetical nominalism divorces authority from the end which constitutes and judges it, it leaves religious life open to distortion and abuse.

Finally, we must also conclude that where the religious life is conceived in dynamic apostolic terms (as it tends to be in this country), a functional asceticism corresponds more perfectly to the spiritual needs of actual religious living. Not that other conceptions of the religious life are not both possible and legitimate: the structure of religious life is sufficiently complex that different facets of it can be emphasized according to the needs of time and circumstance. In this country, however, and at the present time, the very functional structure of our life demands of American religious that they adopt a more functional approach to the problems of religious living in a post-conciliar age. But with this conclusion we must close, for it was with this insight that we originally began our reflections.

APPENDIX I / SOME REFLECTIONS ON THE RELIGIOUS PRIESTHOOD

THE EXPRESSION "to the clergy, religious, and laity" is a standard one in the introduction of many official diocesan documents and speeches. But this courteous convention, while perfectly acceptable in itself, can be misleading to the unreflective; for it seems to imply that a religious is someone utterly distinct both from the clergy and the laity; that, in other words, Catholics are classified as clerics, religious, or laymen. A more accurate statement of the case would be that every religious must be either a cleric or a layman. The category "religious" is not distinct from that of "clergy" and "laity." It embraces the two and is a species of each. Thus, the members of the clergy are either diocesan clergy or religious clergy; the members of the laity are either ordinary laymen or lay religious. The basic confusion here has perhaps been even further confounded by the fact that some orders are composed of both clerical and lay religious. Thus, the fact that both are called "religious" indiscriminately tends to obscure the further fact that the term "religious" is applied analogously to the clerics and laymen who comprise its membership.

Functional Asceticism

We have already discussed the impact of religious vows on the mission of the layman in the Church. We have suggested that their primary impact is to dedicate lay people totally to the service of the Christian community as such, to the accomplishment of some work of importance to the Church as a whole, by incorporating them into an organized apostolic team under the direction of Church authority. We have also suggested that as a result these vows lend to the basic vocation of the layman a new, quasi-sacramental and ecclesial modality and visibility. His vocation as a layman comes to him as an individual primarily through the sacraments of baptism and confirmation (and only secondarily, because optionally, through the sacrament of matrimony). The vocation of the lay religious explicitates visibly and ecclesially (and hence quasi-sacramentally) the universality of the commitment of love present in a layman's original baptismal commitment of faith and hope and in his individual mission of prophetic witness through his confirmation. This the religious vocation accomplishes by lending to that commitment and to that witness a new communal visibility and operational modality.

But what, for the sake of comparison, is the impact (if any) which religious vows have upon the mission of the priest? Is such an impact even possible? On the face of it, it would seem unlikely that religious vows could add anything of note to the priestly vocation as such. For instance, whereas in the case of a layman religious vows can, over and beyond his initial baptismal and confirmational commitment, dedicate him full-time to the service of the Church, a priest, by reason of his very ordination is, as a permanent member of the hierarchy, already dedicated full-time to the work of *diakonia*, of service to the Christian community.

Moreover, priestly service possesses already and of its nature a sacramental value which transcends the quasi-sacramentality of religious vows. For whereas in the case of lay people religious vows do lend to their work of service a new ecclesial visibility, the priest is by contrast already the member of a community of service which is the sacramental extension of the service and authority of his bishop, a service and authority which each priest shares in common with his fellow priests and under the unifying direction of the bishop exercises in co-operation with them. In other words, the unity of purpose underlying the many activities of a diocese and the unifying authority of the bishop who directs them formally constitute, through the sacrament of orders, a priestly community of apostolic service which possesses sacramental and not just quasi-sacramental visibility. The restoration of concelebration in the recent decree on the liturgy issued by Vatican II is at least in part a conscious effort of the *magisterium* to manifest in an explicitly sacramental manner the existing and always implicitly acknowledged fact of an organized sacerdotal community of service in the Church.

151

How, then, do religious vows affect or modify the ordinary priestly life of service? Is any genuine modification even possible? I am inclined to think that it is; but before we attempt to articulate its basic structural outlines, a few reflections on the meaning of the priestly mission itself are perhaps in order.

What, then, is a priest? or perhaps better, who is he? What is his mission in the Church and how does he go about its exercise?

First of all and obviously, the priest is a *man*. And because he is, he shares with other men all of their basic human needs for food, shelter, medical care, companionship, creativity, love, grace, redemption, God.

The priest is also a *male*, with all that this implies physiologically, psychologically, and socially. Hence he is, among other things, inclined to be more aggressive in his emotional makeup than women are generally, and is more inclined to rationality, analysis, and emotional reticence in public than to spontaneous demonstrations of warmth and intuition. His masculinity also creates in him the conscious need to do, to accomplish, to build something of importance in human society at large.

The priest is a *Christian*. That is to say, he is a person who has acknowledged both Christ as the incarnate Son of God, as man's only mediator before our Heavenly Father, and the Church as the historical prolongation of Christ in time through the authority invested in it by him and through the temporal mission of the Holy Spirit.

He is, therefore, one of the baptized, a sacramentally accepted member of a community of worship and practical belief whose mission it is to mediate the grace of Christ to men through a love motivated by an explicit and conscious faith and hope in Christ and in his promises.

The priest is also a *confirmed* Catholic. That is, he is an adult Christian sacramentally sent to bear prophetic, individual witness to the faith and hope which are his in the love of Christ.

The priest is a *deacon;* one, therefore, who has an official authoritative status within the baptized community, an official representative of the bishop before God's people, with power from the bishop to baptize solemnly, to administer the eucharist, to assist at officially and bless the marriages of the faithful, to administer Viaticum to those in danger of death, to proclaim the Sacred Scriptures to the faithful, to administer sacramentals, to officiate at funeral and burial services.

Theologians have always insisted that the office of deacon is contained within the priesthood *eminenter,* that is, that the priestly vocation and mission does not negate but merely expands and extends that of the deacon. For the priest, while retaining his diaconal powers, is by his priestly ordination given a fuller share in the responsibilities of the episcopal mission of sacerdotal service than is the deacon. As a priest he is empowered, over and beyond his diaconal powers, to lead the Christian people in their sacrificial act of worship, to reconcile them to God and to the Christian community against whom they may have sinned, to preach the gospel, and to exercise administrative authority within the community. In other words, priestly ordination dedicates a Christian male sacramentally to the fullest possible service of God's people short of being a bishop.

It is, however, important to reflect that not only one's diaconate but one's humanity, masculinity, and Christianity are also all contained *eminenter* in one's priestly consecration. More specifically, the hierarchical priesthood extends, focuses, and actively fulfills the eucharistic priesthood which is common to all the faithful through their baptismal consecration. Similarly, priestly authority to preach the word of God extends and elevates the prophetic mission of every confirmed, adult Christian by lending to the individual witness of confirmation a new, official ecclesial status. The confirmed Christian bears witness to his faith merely as an individual; but the witness of the priest, while remaining physically that of an individual, is transformed by the sacramental authority vested in him into an official embodiment of the witness of the Christian community as such. Now, once we recall that the sacramental consecration of an individual through baptism and confirmation to a life of Christian witness is in its own order total as well as profoundly incarnational and that it involves the eschatological transformation of the whole person—body and soul—in grace, then the eminent presence within the priestly witness of one's full humanity and masculinity as well as one's Christianity becomes not only clear but religiously and humanly significant. For it is only when we conceive of the priesthood in terms of total transformation in grace and love that we can protect the exercise of the priestly office from the narrow limitations of an excessively nominalistic view of the priestly mission. To the nominalistic mind, the role of the priest is primarily, if not exclusively, cultic. The narrow, legalistic formalism of the nominalist easily leads him to define the priestly mission *exclusively* in terms of those specific actions which the priest and the priest alone is empowered canonically to perform. Thus, for all practical purposes, in a nominalistic world the priest acts truly as a priest only when he is saying Mass, hearing confessions, baptizing, etc. The obvious conclusion which one must draw from such a questionable thesis is that priests spend almost all of their waking hours in the performance of non-priestly tasks "which any layman could do just as well."

Contemporary theology has attempted to counterbalance the narrowness of this excessively juridical view of the priestly life by pointing out that the consecration of the Mass is itself the official public proclamation of the Church's basic message of salvation, and hence that the power to offer Mass dedicates the priest full-time to the official proclamation of the word of God. Moreover, it has been suggested that this double dedication defines the main lines of priestly service within the community. That is to say, in virtue of his ordination the priest becomes pre-eminently a man of God's word. His mission is to interpret to Christians and to the world the meaning of the lived existential witness of committed Catholics both kerygmatically, by preaching founded in study of and prayer over the divine message of salvation, and sacramentally by speaking to men with the graced authority of Christ in the critical salvific situations of their lives. Now, since in the Mass the Church's kerygmatic and sacramental words fuse at the moment of consecration, contemporary theology has also insisted correctly that the fullest exercise of one's priestly function of dual service consists in officiating at the sacrificial worship of the Christian community.

This expanded notion of the dual priestly mission of preaching and sanctification is a theologically solid one and not as revolutionary as its vocabulary might at times seem to suggest. But it can, it seems to me, be profitably supplemented by a few important reflections. For all Christian living (not just the priest's) reaches a high point in the eucharistic act. But at the same time, assisting at Mass no more exhausts the mission of the Catholic layman in the Church and in the world than celebrating it does the priest's.

First of all, it is, I believe, important to reflect that the priestly office is something that is possessed habitually and not simply at the moment of its official, canonical exercise. For without of itself extending canonically the obligation common to all Christians to seek perfection, the priestly character permanently alters one's sacramental status within the Christian community. That is to say, sacramental ordination endows the daily lived witness of the Christian male with a new kind of sacramental visibility even when he is not actually engaged in his official functions of offering sacrifice, preaching, and administering the sacraments. Indeed, it is his permanent power to perform such acts which endows every other human action he performs with a genuinely priestly significance. Why is this so, and what does it mean?

We know that the priest as priest is a mediator; that is to say, in virtue of his sacramental ordination his ecclesial mission is to proclaim sacrificially, kerygmatically, and sacramentally the death of the Lord until he come. Now, because this is so, he stands before God as the sacramental embodiment of God's holy and priestly people, as the consecrated leader and public spokesman of the people of God. As the human focalization of their priestly consecration, the priest is called upon to represent, to re-incarnate, and to mediate to the world the reality of the believing Church in a fashion which truly transcends the witness of the ordinary individual Christian. As we have seen, the ordinary Christian bears witness to his faith only as an individual. The priest, in virtue of his public power to consecrate the eucharist, does so as a sacramental embodiment of and official spokesman for the Christian community as such.

Moreover, because the priestly office is only a partial

157

share in the fullness of the episcopal priesthood, the priest, by virtue of his ordination, also officially mediates and embodies the episcopal presence to the believing Catholic community and in a modified sense to the world at large.

Hence, the priest imparts to every action in which he engages a unique priestly consecration which goes beyond that of the ordinary Christian. The vocation of the layman is, as we have seen, truly incarnational—namely, as an individual to reconsecrate all things to God in and through his faith in Christ. Because the vocation of the priest is also Christian, it too is essentially incarnational as well, but in a manner proportioned to the priestly mission. For the priest is called upon to reconsecrate all things to God in Christ, not merely as an individual, but as the community's sacramental embodiment before God and official spokesman to the world.

There is, therefore, an important reciprocity and complementarity between the Christian witness of the priest and that of the layman. For just as the priest's cultic office presupposes a worshiping community of which he is, under the bishop, head, so too the priest's lived existential witness presupposes the living witness of the Catholic laity in order for it to be completely meaningful to men. For unless the community which he represents in his every action is itself truly holy and dedicated to God, his priestly witness can only appear to men to be the expression of his own personal conviction and nothing else. At

158

the same time, the incarnational witness of the priest lends official and authoritative sanction to the witness of the laity by manifesting visibly that the lay Christian's witness is not merely a matter of *their* individual piety and belief but is the lived profession of the official faith of the Catholic Church as a whole.

It is for this reason that Catholic priests not only can be, but must be, personally involved in everything that a Catholic layman is and does. It is for this reason that lay witness can never simply replace that of a priest, that the Christian witness of both priests and laymen is absolutely necessary in every field of human activity. It is for this reason that the fullness of humanity, with all that that implies, must be present as an inner moment of any truly priestly witness. It is for this reason that there is no area of legitimate human activity which does not cry for a priestly presence to sanction it and give an officially ecclesial dimension to the individual witness of Catholic laymen engaged in it.

It is only when one has thus fully grasped the complete human dimensions of the priestly witness that one can approach the problem of the vocation to the religious priesthood intelligently. Granted, then, the full scope of priestly witness, can the vows of religion add anything to its concrete exercise? If so, what specifically do they add?

Perhaps it would be simplest to begin with the matter of clerical celibacy. The question has come up for considerable discussion recently, frequently enough by per-

sons who are both theologically and historically unin-
formed. It has, of course, always been at least implicit in
Catholic belief that marriage and the priestly state are
compatible and that the celibate life, while most certainly an exceptional grace, need not necessarily go with
priestly orders. It has also been a recognized fact in
Christian tradition that the priestly vocation bears a
special affinity to the celibate life. For instance, one frequently hears it said that in the Oriental Church priests
are allowed to marry, but this is really an inaccurate and
misleading statement of the case. It is not true that priests
are allowed to marry in the Oriental Church. What is true
is that married men are allowed to be ordained priests.
In fact, this legislation concerning marriage among the
clergy sometimes puts an Eastern-rite seminarian who may
wish to marry before ordination in the awkward position
of having to hunt up a wife before he reaches his ordination deadline. Furthermore, the fullness of the priesthood,
which comes with episcopal consecration, is reserved by
law in the Oriental Church exclusively for the celibate.

There are many reasons for thinking that the Oriental
discipline concerning priestly celibacy should be officially
extended to the diocesan clergy of the Latin Church. The
ecumenical advantages alone, in the case of separated
clergymen inclined to reunion, ought to be obvious to all.
But granted the present legislation in the Latin rite,
there would seem to be no basic difference between the
celibate witness of diocesan and of religious clergy. In the

160

case of each, celibacy, while not necessarily connected with their priestly office as such, is clearly a fitting expression and fulfillment of a life of priestly service and dedication.

The vow of poverty, however, introduces a note of genuine difference. Since the priestly life is a life of service to the Christian community, it gives a priest the right to look to that same community for his own material support. Needless to say, his priestly consecration also places upon him the obligation of living conscientiously within economic limits which are compatible with the witness of a life dedicated to the service of others in the name of Christ. But the priestly life as such does not demand of an individual diocesan priest the rededication of any material possessions of his which may exceed what is necessary for his decent survival and apostolic effectiveness in the service of the Church and the community. But this is precisely what a priest does who professes a vow of religious poverty. Hence, when it is truly lived, his vow of poverty becomes a fitting expression of his priestly love and concern for the apostolic needs of others and in an immediate way for the personal needs of the members of his own community, who are vowed like himself to a life of frugal service, and with whom he has all things in common. His vow thus expresses a concern which brings with it obligations that take him beyond the strict demands of his priestly office as such, while it simultaneously prolongs historically the ideals of

161

common life originally practiced in the apostolic church of Jerusalem. As in the case of celibacy, then, his religious vow of poverty is a fitting extension and fulfillment of his priestly *diakonia*.

But as in the case of lay religious, it is, I believe, the vow of obedience which has the greatest existential impact upon the concrete exercise of one's priestly office, for by the vow of obedience a priest becomes the functioning member of a communally organized team of priests dedicated to the task of giving an explicitly corporate priestly witness within the Christian community as a whole. Like the other two vows, then, the vow of obedience extends and completes the basic thrust of the priestly witness of service. Needless to say, the vow of obedience does not incorporate a priest into the sacerdotal community as such; this is done by his sacramental ordination. But by establishing distinct priestly communities of common life and endeavor, it does manifest in a visible, ecclesial manner the essentially communal nature of the priestly brotherhood in a way that cannot be done by the territorially scattered and financially independent diocesan clergy. Moreover, in those religious orders and congregations composed of both priests and laymen, the vow of religious obedience further manifests the important continuity and reciprocity between lay and priestly witness by presenting the Christian community with a living paradigm of clerical and lay co-operation in the work of the apostolate. In addition, in religious orders in the strict sense the vow of obedience provides the people of God with an important application of the collegial structure of the Church. For by his vow of obedience in a religious order, a priest becomes the member of a community of service which prolongs the authority, not of the local bishop, but of the bishop of Rome, who is the head and unifying authority of the whole episcopal college. Therefore, close and brotherly co-operation between diocesan authorities and local superiors of religious orders in their common efforts to serve the people of God, with respect for one another's rights, is an important application and manifestation of the basically collegial structure of the Church's supreme hierarchical authority.

Finally, and perhaps most important from a practical, apostolic point of view, the vow of obedience has a decisive impact on the manner in which a religious priest goes about the practical business of serving the people of God. The involvement of most of the secular clergy in the scattered work of the parishes, plus their financial independence of one another, means that they go about the concrete exercise of their priesthood for the most part as individuals. That is to say, the secular priest has got to be a general practitioner in the apostolate: liturgist, preacher, teacher, social worker, theologian, philosopher, pastor, spiritual director, administrator, fund raiser, and heavens knows what else. The religious priest, on the other hand, by becoming the member of a much larger, apostolically organized priestly community, exercises his

163

priesthood, not as an individual, but as a member of a functioning team of priests. Hence the religious priest is much freer to specialize in one particular area than is his diocesan counterpart. The religious priest-administrator, priest-fund-raiser, priest-teacher, priest-research-specialist, priest-pastor, priest-theologian, priest-preacher, and priest-philosopher will find the explanation of the full priestly character of his individual work only when it is seen in the context of the corporate priestly witness of the community of priests of which he is a member. This is not to say, of course, that many of the tasks now performed by religious priests could not, perhaps, in specific instances, be performed more efficiently by lay religious of the same order or by laymen hired by the order for that purpose. But it is to say that by the corporate character of his priestly witness the religious priest is relieved of the necessity of undertaking many of the variety of tasks which occupy the diocesan clergy. By thus being freed for specialization he is able to cultivate a degree of professional excellence in specific aspects of the priestly ministry which is impossible for most diocesan priests.

It should be clear by now what we meant by saying at the beginning of this appendix that the term "religious" is applied analogously to religious priests and to lay religious. Analogy implies similarity in difference, unity in diversity. In the present instance, the three vows of religion extend and fulfill a basic sacramental mission within the Church in the case of both clerical and lay re-

164

ligious. The analogical difference comes, however, in the particular sacramental mission which the vows extend and complete, namely, that of confirmation or that of holy orders.

Some might still have difficulty in conceiving religious vows as extending, and lending a special ecclesial modality to, priestly orders, since in the case of most religious priests vows precede their ordination chronologically. The problem, however, which we are dealing with here is not one of temporal but one of causal priority. Religious vows dedicate the lay person to a life of service in the Church. But since the priestly ordination of a lay religious changes the official status of his ecclesial service, it also changes the concrete meaning of the witness implied in his religious vows. For while vows may indeed imply a permanent religious commitment, it is the purpose of priestly ordination to reconsecrate the whole of a person to God with sacramental efficacy by dedicating him to a new role of special service in the Church, and hence to reorient the ecclesial modality of his total commitment to God, sacramental or otherwise.

Another concrete conclusion from these reflections is the evident suitability of regular and even daily concelebration in communities of religious priests. Truly, what more fitting liturgical expression and reaffirmation could there be of the peculiarly corporate exercise of the priesthood which is the special mission of the religious priest within the universal Church?

APPENDIX II / DECREE ON THE APPROPRIATE RENEWAL OF THE RELIGIOUS LIFE*

PAUL, BISHOP
SERVANT OF THE SERVANTS OF GOD
TOGETHER WITH THE FATHERS OF THE SACRED COUNCIL
FOR EVERLASTING MEMORY

1. In its Constitution which begins, "The Light of the World," this most sacred Synod has already pointed out how the teaching and example of the Divine Master laid the foundation for a pursuit of perfect charity through the exercise of the evangelical counsels, and how such a pursuit serves as a blazing emblem of the heavenly kingdom. In this present document, the Synod intends to deal with the life and rules of those institutes whose members profess chastity, poverty, and obedience, and to make provisions for their needs as the tenor of the times indicates.

* Excerpts from the Constitutions, Declarations, and Decrees of the Ecumenical Council are taken from *The Documents of Vatican II*, published by Guild Press, America Press, and Association Press, and copyrighted 1966 by The America Press. Used by permission.

From the very infancy of the Church, there have existed men and women who strove to follow Christ more freely and imitate Him more nearly by the practice of the evangelical counsels. Each in his own way, these souls have led a life dedicated to God. Under the influence of the Holy Spirit, many of them pursued a solitary life, or founded religious families to which the Church willingly gave the welcome and approval of her authority.

And so it happened by divine plan that a wonderful variety of religious communities grew up. This variety contributed mightily toward making the Church experienced in every good deed (cf. 2 Tim. 3:17) and ready for a ministry of service in building up Christ's body (cf. Eph. 4:12). Not only this, but adorned by the various gifts of her children, the Church became radiant like a bride made beautiful for her spouse (cf. Apoc. 21:2); and through her God's manifold wisdom could reveal itself (cf. Eph. 3:10).

But whatever the diversity of their spiritual endowments, all who are called by God to practice the evangelical counsels, and who do so faithfully, devote themselves in a special way to the Lord. They imitate Christ the virgin and the poor man (cf. Mt. 8:20; Lk. 9:58), who, by an obedience which carried Him even to death on the cross (cf. Phil. 2:8), redeemed men and made them holy. As a consequence, impelled by a love which the Holy Spirit has poured into their hearts (cf. Rom. 5:5), these Christians spend themselves ever increasingly

170

for Christ, and for His body the Church (cf. Col. 1:24).

Hence the more ardently they unite themselves to Christ through a self-surrender involving their entire lives, the more vigorous becomes the life of the Church and the more abundantly her apostolate bears fruit.

A life consecrated by a profession of the counsels is of surpassing value. Such a life has a necessary role to play in the circumstances of the present age. That this kind of life and its contemporary role may achieve greater good for the Church, this sacred Synod issues the following decrees. They concern only the general principles which must underlie an appropriate renewal of the life and rules of religious communities. These principles apply also to societies living a community life without the exercise of vows, and to secular institutes, though the special character of both groups is to be maintained. After the Council, the competent authority will be obliged to enact particular laws opportunely spelling out and applying what is legislated here.

2. The appropriate renewal of religious life involves two simultaneous processes: (1) a continuous return to the sources of all Christian life and to the original inspiration behind a given community and (2) an adjustment of the community to the changed conditions of the times. It is according to the following principles that such renewal should go forward under the influence of the Holy Spirit and the guidance of the Church.

a) Since the fundamental norm of the religious life is a following of Christ as proposed by the gospel, such is to be regarded by all communities as their supreme law.

b) It serves the best interests of the Church for communities to have their own special character and purpose. Therefore loyal recognition and safekeeping should be accorded to the spirit of founders, as also to all the particular goals and wholesome traditions which constitute the heritage of each community.

c) All communities should participate in the life of the Church. According to its individual character, each should make its own and foster in every possible way the enterprises and objectives of the Church in such fields as these: the scriptural, liturgical, doctrinal, pastoral, ecumenical, missionary, and social.

d) Communities should promote among their members a suitable awareness of contemporary human conditions and of the needs of the Church. For if their members can combine the burning zeal of an apostle with wise judgments, made in the light of faith, concerning the circumstances of the modern world, they will be able to come to the aid of men more effectively.

e) Since the religious life is intended above all else to lead those who embrace it to an imitation of Christ and to union with God through the profession of the evangelical counsels, the fact must be honestly faced that even the most desirable changes made on behalf of contemporary needs will fail of their purpose unless a

172

renewal of spirit gives life to them. Indeed such an interior renewal must always be accorded the leading role even in the promotion of exterior works.

3. The manner of living, praying, and working should be suitably adapted to the physical and psychological conditions of today's religious and also, to the extent required by the nature of each community, to the needs of the apostolate, the requirements of a given culture, the social and economic circumstances anywhere, but especially in missionary territories.

The way in which communities are governed should also be re-examined in the light of these same standards.

For this reason constitutions, directories, custom books, books of prayers and ceremonies, and similar compilations are to be suitably revised and brought into harmony with the documents of this sacred Synod. This task will require the suppression of outmoded regulations.

4. Successful renewal and proper adaptation cannot be achieved unless every member of a community cooperates.

In the work of appropriate renewal, it is the responsibility of competent authorities alone, especially of general chapters, to issue norms, to pass laws, and to allow for a right amount of prudent experimentation, though in all such matters, according to the norm of law, the approval of the Holy See and of local Ordinaries must be given when it is required. In decisions which involve the future of an institute as a whole, superiors should in appropriate manner consult the members and give them a hearing.

For the suitable renewal of convents of nuns, their wishes and recommendations can also be ascertained from meetings of federations or from other assemblies lawfully convoked.

Let all bear in mind, however, that the hope of renewal must be lodged in a more diligent observance of rule and of constitution rather than in a multiplication of individual laws.

5. The members of each community should recall above everything else that by their profession of the evangelical counsels they have given answer to a divine call to live for God alone not only by dying to sin (cf. Rom. 6:11) but also by renouncing the world. They have handed over their entire lives to God's service in an act of special consecration which is deeply rooted in their baptismal consecration and which provides an ampler manifestation of it.

Inasmuch as their self-dedication has been accepted by the Church, they should realize that they are committed to her service as well.

The fact that they are in God's service should ignite and fan within them the exercise of virtues, especially humility, obedience, courage, and chastity. Through them

174

they share spiritually in Christ's self-surrender (cf. Phil.
2:7-8) and in His life (cf. Rom. 8:1-13).

Therefore, in fidelity to their profession and in renunciation of all things for the sake of Christ (cf. Mk. 10:28),
let religious follow Him (cf. Mt. 19:21) as their one
necessity (cf. Lk. 10:42). Let them listen to His words
(cf. Lk. 10:39) and be preoccupied with His work (cf.
1 Cor. 7:32).

To this end, as they seek God before all things and
only Him, the members of each community should combine contemplation with apostolic love. By the former
they adhere to God in mind and heart; by the latter they
strive to associate themselves with the work of redemption and to spread the Kingdom of God.

6. Those who profess the evangelical counsels love and
seek before all else that God who took the initiative in
loving us (cf. 1 Jn. 4:10); in every circumstance they aim
to develop a life hidden with Christ in God (cf. Col. 3:3).
Such dedication gives rise and urgency to the love of
one's neighbor for the world's salvation and the upbuilding of the Church. From this love the very practice of
the evangelical counsels takes life and direction.

Therefore, drawing on the authentic sources of Christian spirituality, let the members of communities ener-
getically cultivate the spirit of prayer and the practice of
it. In the first place they should take the sacred Scriptures in hand each day by way of attaining "the ex-

celling knowledge of Jesus Christ" (Phil. 3:8) through reading these divine writings and meditating on them. They should enact the sacred liturgy, especially the most holy mystery of the Eucharist, with hearts and voices attuned to the Church; here is a most copious source of nourishment for the spiritual life.

Fed thus at the table of the divine law and of the sacred altar, they can bring a brother's love to the members of Christ, and a son's love to their revered pastors; thus they can live and think with the Church to an ever-increasing degree, and spend themselves completely on her mission.

7. Members of those communities which are totally dedicated to contemplation give themselves to God alone in solitude and silence and through constant prayer and ready penance. No matter how urgent may be the needs of the active apostolate, such communities will always have a distinguished part to play in Christ's Mystical Body, where "all members have not the same function" (Rom. 12:4). For they offer God a choice sacrifice of praise. They brighten God's people with the richest splendors of sanctity. By their example they motivate this people; by imparting a hidden, apostolic fruitfulness, they make this people grow. Thus they are the glory of the Church and an overflowing fountain of heavenly graces. Nevertheless, their manner of living should be revised according to the aforementioned principles and standards

of appropriate renewal, though their withdrawal from the world and the practices of their contemplative life should be maintained at their holiest.

8. There exist within the Church a great number of clerical and lay institutes devoted to various aspects of the apostolate. They have contributions to make which are as various as the graces given them: some exercise a ministry of service, some teach doctrine, some encourage through exhortation, some give in simplicity, or bring cheerfulness to the sorrowful (cf. Rom. 12:5–8). "Now there are varieties of gifts, but the same Spirit" (1 Cor. 12:4).

In such communities the very nature of the religious life requires apostolic action and services, since a sacred ministry and a special work of charity have been consigned to them by the Church and must be discharged in her name. Hence the entire religious life of the members of these communities should be penetrated by an apostolic spirit, as their entire apostolic activity should be animated by a religious spirit. Therefore, in order that members may above all respond to their vocation of following Christ and may serve Christ Himself in His members, their apostolic activity should result from an intimate union with Him. In this way it will happen that love for God and neighbor will itself be nurtured.

These communities, then, should skillfully harmonize their observances and practices with the needs of the

177

apostolate to which they are dedicated. But inasmuch as the religious life which is committed to apostolic works takes on many forms, a necessary diversity will have to distinguish its path to a suitable renewal, and members of the various communities will have to be sustained in living for Christ's service by means which are proper and fitting for themselves.

9. In the East and in the West, the venerable institution of monastic life should be faithfully preserved, and should grow ever-increasingly radiant with its own authentic spirit. Through the long course of the centuries, this institution has proved its merits splendidly to the Church and to human society. The main task of monks is to render to the Divine Majesty a service at once simple and noble, within the monastic confines. This they do either by devoting themselves entirely to divine worship in a life that is hidden, or by lawfully taking up some apostolate or works of Christian charity. While safeguarding the proper identity of each institution, let monasteries be renewed in their ancient and beneficial traditions, and so adapt them to the modern needs of souls that monasteries will be seedbeds of growth for the Christian people.

There are religious communities which by rule or constitution closely join the apostolic life with choral prayer and monastic observances. Let these groups, too, so harmonize their manner of life with the requirements of the apostolate belonging to them that they still faithfully

178

preserve their form of life, for it is one which serves the highest welfare of the Church.

10. The lay religious life, for both men and women, constitutes a state which of itself is one of total dedication to the profession of the evangelical counsels. This sacred Synod highly esteems such a life, since it serves the pastoral work of the Church so usefully by educating the young, caring for the sick, and discharging other services. The Council supports such religious in their vocation, and entreats them to adapt their life to modern needs.

This sacred Synod declares that there is no objection to religious congregations of brothers admitting some members to holy orders, to supply needed priestly ministrations for their own houses, provided that the lay character of the congregation remains unchanged and that it is the general chapter that makes the decision.

11. Secular institutes are not religious communities but they carry with them in the world a profession of the evangelical counsels which is genuine and complete, and recognized as such by the Church. This profession confers a consecration on men and women, laity and clergy, who reside in the world. For this reason they should chiefly strive for total self-dedication to God, one inspired by perfect charity. These institutes should preserve their proper and particular character, a secular one, so that

they may everywhere measure up successfully to that apostolate which they were designed to exercise, and which is both in the world and, in a sense, of the world.

Yet they should surely realize that they cannot acquit themselves of so immense a task unless their members are skillfully trained in matters both human and divine, and can thus be a genuine leaven in the world for strengthening and enlarging Christ's body. Therefore directors should give especially serious care to the spiritual training of members and to the promotion of more advanced formation as well.

12. That chastity which is practiced "on behalf of the heavenly Kingdom" (Mt. 19:12), and which religious profess, deserves to be esteemed as a surpassing gift of grace. For it liberates the human heart in a unique way (cf. 1 Cor. 7:32-35) and causes it to burn with greater love for God and all mankind. It is therefore an outstanding token of heavenly riches, and also a most suitable way for religious to spend themselves readily in God's service and in works of the apostolate. Religious thereby give witness to all Christ's faithful of that wondrous marriage between the Church and Christ her only spouse, a union which has been established by God and will be fully manifested in the world to come.

Hence, as they strive to live their profession faithfully, religious do well to lodge their faith in the words of the Lord; trusting in God's help rather than presuming on their own resources, let them practice mortification and custody of the senses. They should take advantage of those natural helps which favor mental and bodily health. As a result they will not be influenced by those erroneous claims which present complete continence as impossible or as harmful to human development. In addition a certain spiritual instinct should lead them to spurn everything likely to imperil chastity. Above all, everyone should remember—superiors especially—that chastity has stronger safeguards in a community when true fraternal love thrives among its members.

Since the observance of total continence intimately involves the deeper inclinations of human nature, candidates should not undertake the profession of chastity nor be admitted to its profession except after a truly adequate testing period and only if they have the needed degree of psychological and emotional maturity. They should not only be warned of the dangers confronting chastity, but be trained to make a celibate life consecrated to God part of the richness of their whole personality.

13. Poverty voluntarily embraced in imitation of Christ provides a witness which is highly esteemed, especially today. Let religious painstakingly cultivate such poverty, and give it new expressions if need be. By it a man shares in the poverty of Christ, who became poor for our sake when before He had been rich, that we might be enriched by His poverty (cf. 2 Cor. 8:9; Mt. 8:20).

Functional Asceticism

Religious poverty requires more than limiting the use of possessions to the consent of superiors; members of a community ought to be poor in both fact and spirit, and have their treasures in heaven (cf. Mt. 6:20).

In discharging his duty, each religious should regard himself as subject to the common law of labor. While making necessary provisions for their livelihood and undertakings, religious should brush aside all undue concern and entrust themselves to the providence of the heavenly Father (cf. Mt. 6:25).

In their constitutions, religious communities can allow their members to renounce any inheritance which they have acquired or are due to acquire.

Depending on the circumstances of their location, communities as such should aim at giving a kind of corporate witness to their own poverty. Let them willingly contribute something from their own resources to the other needs of the Church, and to the support of the poor, whom religious should love with the tenderness of Christ (cf. Mt. 19:21; 25:34-46; Jas. 2:15-16; 1 Jn. 3:17). Provinces and houses of a religious community should share their resources with one another, those which are better supplied assisting those which suffer need.

To the degree that their rules and constitutions permit, religious communities can rightly possess whatever is necessary for their temporal life and their mission. Still, let them avoid every appearance of luxury, of excessive wealth, and accumulation of possessions.

182

14. Through the profession of obedience, religious offer to God a total dedication of their own wills as a sacrifice of themselves; they thereby unite themselves with greater steadiness and security to the saving will of God. In this way they follow the pattern of Jesus Christ, who came to do the Father's will (cf. Jn. 4:34; 5:30; Heb. 10:7; Ps. 39:9). "Taking the nature of a slave" (Phil. 2:7), He learned obedience from His sufferings (cf. Heb. 5:8). Under the influence of the Holy Spirit, religious submit themselves to their superiors, whom faith presents as God's representatives, and through whom they are guided into the service of all their brothers in Christ. Thus did Christ Himself out of submission to the Father minister to the brethren and surrender His life as a ransom for many (cf. Mt. 20:28; Jn. 10:14–18). In this way, too, religious assume a firmer commitment to the ministry of the Church and labor to achieve the mature measure of the fullness of Christ (cf. Eph. 4:13).

Therefore, in a spirit of faith and of love for God's will, let religious show humble obedience to their superiors in accord with the norms of rule and constitution. Realizing that they are giving service to the upbuilding of Christ's body according to God's design, let them bring to the execution of commands and to the discharge of assignments entrusted to them the resources of their minds and wills, and their gifts of nature and grace. Lived in this manner, religious obedience will not diminish the dignity of the human person but will rather lead it to maturity in consequence of that enlarged freedom which belongs to the sons of God.

For his part, as one who will render an account for the souls entrusted to him (cf. Heb. 13:17), each superior should himself be docile to God's will in the exercise of his office. Let him use his authority in a spirit of service for the brethren, and manifest thereby the charity with which God loves them. Governing his subjects as God's own sons, and with regard for their human personality, a superior will make it easier for them to obey gladly. Therefore he must make a special point of leaving them appropriately free with respect to the sacrament of penance and direction of conscience. Let him give the kind of leadership which will encourage religious to bring an active and responsible obedience to the offices they shoulder and the activities they undertake. Therefore a superior should listen willingly to his subjects and encourage them to make a personal contribution to the welfare of the community and of the Church. Not to be weakened, however, is the superior's authority to decide what must be done and to require the doing of it.

Let chapters and councils faithfully acquit themselves of the governing role given to them; each should express in its own way the fact that all members of the community have a share in the welfare of the whole community and a responsibility for it.

15. The Primitive Church provided an example of community life when the multitude of believers were of one

heart and one mind (cf. Acts 4:32), and found nourishment in the teaching of the gospel and in the sacred liturgy, especially the Eucharist. Let such a life continue in prayerfulness and a sharing of the same spirit (cf. Acts 2:42). As Christ's members living fraternally together, let them excel one another in showing respect (cf. Rom. 12:10), and let each carry the other's burdens (cf. Gal. 6:2). For thanks to God's love poured into hearts by the Holy Spirit (cf. Rom. 5:5), a religious community is a true family gathered together in the Lord's name and rejoicing in His presence (cf. Mt. 18:20). For love is the fulfillment of the law (cf. Rom. 13:10) and the bond of perfection (cf. Col. 3:14); where it exists we know we have been taken from death to life (cf. 1 Jn. 3:14). In fact, brotherly unity shows that Christ has come (cf. Jn. 13:35; 17:21); from it results great apostolic influence.

To strengthen the bond of brotherhood between members of a community, those who are called lay brothers, assistants, or some other name, should be brought into the heart of its life and activities. Unless the state of affairs suggests otherwise, care must be taken to produce in women's communities a single category of sister. Then there may be retained only such distinction between persons as is demanded by the diversity of the works for which sisters are destined by a special call from God or by particular aptitude.

According to the norms of their constitutions, monasteries and communities of men which are not exclusively lay in their character can admit both clergy and laity on the same basis and with equal rights and duties, excepting those which result from ordination.

16. The papal cloister for nuns totally dedicated to contemplation is to be retained. Still, it should be modified according to the conditions of time and place, and outdated customs done away with. In such matters, consideration should be given to the wishes of the monasteries themselves.

Other nuns institutionally devoted to external works of the apostolate should be exempt from papal cloister so that they can better discharge the apostolic tasks assigned to them. They should, however, maintain the kind of cloister required by their constitutions.

17. Since they are signs of a consecrated life, religious habits should be simple and modest, at once poor and becoming. They should meet the requirements of health and be suited to the circumstances of time and place as well as to the services required by those who wear them. Habits of men and women which do not correspond to those norms are to be changed.

18. The suitable renewal of religious communities depends very largely on the training of their members. Therefore religious men other than clerics, and religious women as well, should not be assigned to apostolic works

immediately after the novitiate. In suitable residences and in a fitting manner, let them continue their training in the religious life and the apostolate, in doctrine and technical matters, even to the extent of winning appropriate degrees.

Lest the adaptations of religious life to the needs of our time be merely superficial, and lest those who by constitution pursue the external apostolate prove unequal to the fulfillment of their task, religious should be properly instructed, according to the intellectual gifts and personal endowments of each, in the prevailing manners of contemporary social life, and in its characteristic ways of feeling and thinking. If such training is harmoniously coordinated it will contribute to integrity of life on the part of religious.

Throughout their lives religious should labor earnestly to perfect their spiritual, doctrinal, and professional development. As far as possible, superiors should provide them with the opportunity, the resources, and the time to do so.

It also devolves upon superiors to see that the best persons are chosen for directors, spiritual guides, and professors, and that they are carefully trained.

19. When there is a question of establishing new communities, serious thought must be given to the need for them, or at least to their eminent usefulness, and also to the likelihood that they will prosper. Otherwise, lack of

187

caution will give rise to communities which serve no purpose or are deprived of sufficient vitality.

When the Church has newly taken root, special attention should be given to the establishment and development of fresh forms of religious life. These should take into account the natural endowments and the manners of the people, and also local customs and circumstances.

20. Communities should faithfully maintain and fulfill their proper activities. Yet, they should make adjustments in them according to the needs of time and place and in favor of what will benefit the universal Church and individual dioceses. To this end they should resort to suitable techniques, including modern ones, and abandon whatever activities are today less in keeping with the spirit of the community and its authentic character.

The missionary spirit should be thoroughly maintained in religious communities, and, according to the character of each one, given a modern expression. In this way the preaching of the gospel among all peoples can be done more successfully.

21. If after consulting the appropriate Ordinaries, the Holy See decides that certain communities or monasteries no longer offer any reasonable hope of flourishing, these should be forbidden thereafter to accept novices. If it can be done, they should be absorbed by a more vigorous community or monastery which approximates their own purpose and spirit.

22. Where opportunity and the Holy See permit, independent communities and monasteries should work towards making a federation of themselves if they belong in some sense to the same religious family; or, if their constitutions and customs are practically the same and a kindred spirit animates them, they should try to form a union, especially when of themselves they are excessively small; or let them enter into an association if they engage in external activities of an identical or similar nature.

23. Favor is to be shown to conferences or councils of major superiors which have been established by the Holy See. These can make splendid contributions to several goals: helping individual communities fulfill their purpose more adequately; fostering more successful cooperation on behalf of the Church; distributing workers in a given territory more advantageously; and working on affairs of common concern to religious communities.

Where the exercise of the apostolate is involved, appropriate coordination and collaboration with episcopal conferences should be established.

Similar conferences can also be set up for secular institutes.

24. Priests and Catholic teachers should make serious efforts on behalf of religious vocations, so that a new supply may be at hand for meeting the Church's needs adequately. Candidates should be appropriately and carefully selected. Ordinary sermons should treat more often

of the evangelical counsels and the choice of the religious state. Parents should develop and protect religious vocations in the hearts of their children by training them to behave like Christians.

Communities have the right to spread knowledge of themselves by way of attracting vocations, and to seek out candidates as well. Only, they should do so with proper prudence, adhering to the norms set down by the Holy See and the local bishop.

Religious should not forget that the good example of their own lives affords the highest recommendation for their community, and the most appealing invitation to embrace the religious life.

25. The communities for which these norms of appropriate renewal are decreed should react with a willing spirit to their divine calling and their contemporary mission in the Church. This sacred Synod has high regard for the character of their life—virginal, poor, and obedient—of which Christ the Lord Himself is the model. The Council places steady hope in the immense fruitfulness of their labors, both the unseen ones and the obvious.

Let all religious therefore spread throughout the whole world the good news of Christ by the integrity of their faith, their love for God and neighbor, their devotion to the Cross, and their hope of future glory. Thus will their witness be seen by all, and our Father in heaven will be glorified (cf. Mt. 5:16). Thus, too, with the prayerful aid of that most loving Virgin Mary, God's Mother, "whose life is a rule of life for all," religious communities will experience a daily growth in numbers, and will yield a richer harvest of fruits that bring salvation.

Each and every one of the things set forth in this Decree has won the consent of the Fathers of this most sacred Council. We, too, by the apostolic authority conferred on us by Christ, join with the Venerable Fathers in approving, decreeing, and establishing these things in the Holy Spirit, and we direct that what has thus been enacted in synod be published in God's glory.

Rome, at St. Peter's, October 28, 1965

I, Paul, Bishop of the Catholic Church

There follow the signatures of the Fathers.